D0686547

# His Own Words:

Translation and Analysis of the Writings of
Dr. Ayman Al Zawahiri

Includes
Knights Under the Prophet's Banner

And

Selected Post September 11, 2001
Communiqués and Messages

Translation and Analysis

By

Laura Mansfield

Copyright 2006 by Laura Mansfield

All rights reserved. No part of this book may be used or reproduced in any manner whatsoever without written permission, except in the case of brief quotations embodied in critical articles or reviews.

Published 2006
by TLG Publications
Printed in the United States of America
ISBN: 978-1-84728-880-6

# His Own Words:
# Translation and Analysis of the Writings of
# Dr. Ayman Al Zawahiri

## Includes
## Knights Under the Prophet's Banner

## Translation and Analysis

## By

## Laura Mansfield

If there must be trouble let it be in my day, that my
child may have peace.

Thomas Paine

For everything there is a season,
And a time for every matter under heaven:
A time to be born, and a time to die;
A time to plant, and a time to pluck up what is
planted;
A time to kill, and a time to heal;
A time to break down, and a time to build up;
A time to weep, and a time to laugh;
A time to mourn, and a time to dance;
A time to throw away stones, and a time to
gather stones together;
A time to embrace, And a time to refrain from
embracing;
A time to seek, and a time to lose;
A time to keep, and a time to throw away;
A time to tear, and a time to sew;
A time to keep silence, and a time to speak;
A time to love, and a time to hate,
A time for war, and a time for peace.

Ecclesiastes 3:1-8

# About the Author

Laura Mansfield is a writer and commentator on issues regarding the Middle East, Islam, and Radical Islamic Terrorism.

Laura has over 20 years of experience dealing with issues pertaining to the Middle East. She is fluent in written and spoken Arabic, and has an excellent understanding of the complex cultural, religious, and historical issues.

She spent nearly 7 years living and working in the region, for a wide range of clients including the United States Embassy, the United States Agency for International Development, and various international corporations. She was active in the embassy warden system, acting as a liaison between the Embassy security office and her employer during the days of the Beirut hijacking.

Subscribers to her Strategic Translations and Analysis service include major libraries in the US, the UK, Germany, and Italy; various US and UK governmental and intelligence agencies; law enforcement agencies in the US, UK, Italy, and Germany; and many Fortune 500 companies.

Laura has been a guest on both CNN and CNN International, as well as Fox News,

Fox News UK, the BBC, and CBN (Canadian Broadcasting Network).

She is a regular guest on KGO Radio News in San Francisco., and has been a regular guest on the syndicated late night talk show, America at Night, providing a weekly terrorism update.

Her commentary has also been featured on WDEL, WFED, WTOP, the Laurie Roth Show, the Tom Bauerle Show, and the Carl Wigglesworth Show. She has appeared on numerous occasions on Israel National Radio.

She has been cited as an expert by many major media outlets including World Net Daily, FrontPage Magazine, the New York Times, the Washington Post, and the Sunday Mirror UK.

Laura has been featured in the Arabic speaking world as well for her cutting edge analysis and her language skills. Last year, Laura was the subject of a prominent feature on Arabiya TV.

She is a regular subject matter consultant for news agencies in the UK, the US, Germany, Italy, and Israel.

Laura is also the author of the book **One Nation Under Allah: The Islamic Invasion of America** and **Inshallah: My Journey Into Radical Islam, and My Escape**.

Laura's writing and current analysis can also be seen at her website at http://www.lauramansfield.com/

# Dedication

This book is dedicated with love to my children and to my husband.

Without their help and support it would not have been possible.

I love you all very much.

# Acknowledgements

Special thanks to my friend and mentor, Jayna Davis, for all her support and encouragement, and for never letting me give up.

To my friends Jeff Epstein and his wife – thank you so much for all of your support and encouragement.

I'd like to say a special thank you to my friends Susan, Peggy, Victoria, Karen, and Lisa.

To my friend Archangel, who hunts the web day and night for Al Qaeda publications and videos, thank you!

To my children, who by now dread the announcement of a new Al Qaeda tape, because they know Mom will be busy translating for the next day or so – thank you for putting up with me. I love you very much!

And most of all to my husband – a special thank you for all the nights you've had to eat leftovers, for the evenings and weekends when you've been truly jihadi-bored. I love you dearly.

*By Laura Mansfield*

---

## Introduction

Egyptian physician Ayman Zawahiri is widely credited with being the brains behind the terror infrastructure of Al Qaeda. He is often labeled as the Al Qaeda second in command, but in many ways he as critical to the daily functioning of Al Qaeda as Osama Bin Laden is, if not more so.

Since the September 11, 2001 attacks on the United States, Zawahiri has taken the forefront in communications to what Al Qaeda refers to as the Islamic Ummah – the family of believers in the strict brand of Islam that Al Qaeda promotes. In fact, for every audio and video tape that Bin Laden had released during that time period, Zawahiri released 3.

In 2001, Zawahiri published a book called "Knights Under the Prophet's Banner", a treatise which provides considerable insight into the mind of the Al Qaeda organization.

Until now, this book was only available in Arabic.

However, I believe it provides information that is critical to anyone who wants to understand Al Qaeda.

In much the same way that Adolf Hitler with Mein Kampf, Dr. Ayman Zawahiri has laid out his ideology, and provided a clear roadmap as to Al Qaeda's plans for the coming decade.

**Knights Under the Prophets Banner** was written in 2001. Looking back at the years since it was written, we can see how Al Qaeda has followed the plans outlined by Zawahiri.

It has been said that those who do not learn from history are doomed to repeat it.

Al Qaeda has historically told us what they are going to do, and then proceeded to do it. **Knights Under the Prophets Banner** goes into more depth than any other Al Qaeda publication.

I have translated and published this in English so that the English-speaking world can see what Al Qaeda's plans are for us and the rest of the world.

# Part I

# Knights Under the Prophets Banner

**By Dr. Ayman al Zawahiri**
*(translation by Laura Mansfield)*

*By Laura Mansfield*

# Knights Under the Prophets Banner

## By Dr. Ayman al Zawahiri
### *(translation by Laura Mansfield)*

I have written this book to fulfill a duty entrusted to me towards our generation and future generations. Perhaps I will not be able to write later on in the midst of these worrying circumstances and changing conditions.

I have written this book although I expect no publisher to publish it or a distributor to distribute it.

It is important to me at first to answer three questions about this book. Who wrote it? Why did he write it? For Whom did he write it?

Who am I, the man who wrote this book? I am a man with a connection with the mujahideen and have forged a bond with them. I hope to spend whatever is left of my life in serving the cause of Islam in its ferocious war against the tyrants of the new Crusade. I wrote it while being a wanted man, a fugitive.

Why did I write this book? Why at this particular time? What benefit will it bring to the reader? What can it add to the large flood of daily books? The answer is: This book was written in an attempt to revive the Muslim nation's awareness of its role and duty, its importance, and the duties that it needs to perform. The book also explains the extent of the new Crusaders' enmity to the Muslim nation and this nation's need to see the dividing line between its enemies and loyal subjects.

We need to admit that successful attempts have been made to infiltrate our ranks, that these attempts have attracted some of our prominent names, and our enemies have added them to the crowds that serve their purposes, including the writers of falsehoods, those who exploit principles for personal gain, and those who sell their fatwas (religious rulings) as commodities.

This book has been written as a warning to the forces of evil that lie in wait for this nation. We tell them: The nation is drawing closer every day to its victory over you and is about to inflict its rightful punishment (qasas) on you step by step; your battle against this nation is destined to lead to inevitable defeat for yourselves, and all your efforts are no more than an attempt to delay this nation's victory, not to prevent it.

This is the stage of the global battle, now that the forces of the disbelievers have united against the mujahideen.

The battle today cannot be fought on a regional level without taking into account the global hostility towards us.

In writing this book, I have sought to explain some of the features of the currently raging epic battle, and to alert the readers to the hidden and open enemies, their wolves and their foxes, so that they can be on their guard against the brigands who wish to rob them.

They possess a quality that their enemies cannot hope to acquire. They are the people who most eloquently bear witness to their God's power, Who has given them a strength drawn from His Own strength, until they have turned from a scattered few who possess little and know little, into a power that is feared and that threatens the stability of the new world order.

I have also written this book to perform my duty to our generation and the generations that will follow. Perhaps I will not be able to write more amid all these worrying circumstances and changing conditions that remind me of Al-Mutanabbi's words:

*A stranger without friends in every town he visits; whenever the need becomes greater, the number of those who can help grows smaller.*

I wrote this book so that it will be read by two kinds of people. The first is the intellectual group, the second the mujahideen group. For this reason I have sought to write it in a clear, simple style and avoided the methods and inferences of specialists.

I could not gather enough documentation necessary for this kind of analytical writing because of the lack of stability in Afghanistan.. Furthermore, the author possesses only his testimony which he cannot provide in detail because many of its characters are still in the midst of battle, and many of its events are still interacting in the field.

I am an emigrant fugitive, who gives his backing to other emigrants and mujahideen; he strengthens their resolve, and reminds them of God's bountiful mercy.

The name "Arab Afghans" is a tendentious description because these mujahideen have never been solely Arab, but mujahideen from all parts of the Islamic world, though the Arabs have been a distinctive element in this group.

These young men have revived a religious duty of which the nation had long been deprived, by fighting in Afghanistan, Kashmir, Bosnia-Herzegovina, and Chechnya.

In the training camps and on the battlefronts against the Russians, the Muslim youths developed a broad awareness and a fuller realization of the conspiracy that is being weaved. They developed an understanding based on shari'ah of the enemies of Islam, the renegades, and their collaborators.

Of course the world order was not going to accept the existence of this growing phenomenon of Arab Afghans that is rebellious against it and a threat to its existence, especially after Western and, later, communist occupation made continuous efforts over an entire century to subjugate the Muslim nations with regulations, laws, forged elections, states of emergency, and immigration and naturalization laws.

The reaction to the Arab Afghans began with their expulsion from Pakistan in the early 1990s and reached its peak in 1992.

It is an irony of fate that Pakistan's secular government expelled to an unknown destination the very persons who had defended its borders. On the Afghan side of the Torkham border crossing between Pakistan and Afghanistan stands a cemetery that contains the remains of more than 100 Arab mujahideen from Afghanistan. It stands as a witness to the Pakistani Government's attitude to those who defended its borders against the communist threat.

Now the Arab Afghans have become dispersed throughout the world. Some are refugees, some immigrants, some living in hiding, some captives, some dead, some carrying arms to defend yet another Muslim front, and some have despaired and are trying to return to a normal life after seeing the enemies' viciousness and the ferocity with which they pursue the mujahideen.

The Arab and Western media are responsible for distorting the image of the Arab Afghans by portraying them as obssessed half-mad people who have rebelled against the United States that once trained and financed them. This lie was repeated more frequently after the Arab Afghans returned to Afghanistan for the second time in the mid-1990s in the wake of the bombing of the US embassies in Nairobi and Dar el Salam.

The purpose of the distortion campaign against the Arab Afghans is clear and obvious, namely, the wish of the United States to deprive the Muslim nation of the honor of heroism and to pretend to be saying: Those whom you consider heroes are actually my creation and my mercenaries who rebelled against me when I stopped backing them.

This lie is self-contradictory. If the Arab Afghans are a US creation, why did the United States seek to expel them over a period of two years?

The truth that everyone should learn is that the United States did not give one penny in aid to the mujahideen.

The financial aid to the Afghans from popular Arab sources amounted to $200 million in 10 years.

If the Arab Afghans are the mercenaries of the United States who have now rebelled against it, why is the United States unable to buy them back now? Would not buying them be more economical and less costly than the security and prevention budget that it is paying to defend itself now?

My travel to faraway countries was predestined.

[Translator's note: Zawahiri had been filling in on a temporary basis for a physician colleague in a clinic in Cairo's Al-Sayyidah Zaynab neighborhood that was run by the Islamic Medical Society, a society administered by the Muslim Brotherhood. The clinic's director, a Muslim Brother, asked him to go to Afghanistan to help in a relief effort. Al-Zawahiri says that he was one of three doctors who arrived in the border city of Peshawar in the summer of 1980, to participate in relief work among the Afghan refugees. ]

The basic objective was to attack the US Embassy in Islamabad, but if that proved difficult to do, then to strike at any other US target in Pakistan. However, following intensive and detailed surveillance, we discovered that bombing the US Embassy was beyond our capability.

The opportunity to go to Afghanistan was a gift handed on a gold platter. I was always searching for a secure base for jihadist activity in Egypt because the members of the fundamentalist movement were the target of repeated security crackdowns.

My old friend Abu-Ubaydah al-Banshiri, former military commander of al-Qaeda forces, who drowned in Lake Victoria in 1996 said: "It is as if 100 years were added to my life when I came to Afghanistan."

Kamal al-Sananiri, the official in charge of the Muslim Brotherhood's "Special Order Group" died in prison under the torture of Hasan Abu-Basha, director of the State Security Investigation Department at that time, who went on to become interior minister.

Although I never knew Al-Sananiri personally, the evidence of his presence in Peshawar and Afghanistan used to precede us wherever we went." Abu-Talal al-Qasimi Tal'at Fu'ad Qasim, spokesman for the Islamic Group, says that the United States abducted Al-Sananiri in Croatia and handed him over to Egypt in the mid-1980s. Abu-Talal used to occupy a jail cell next to Al-Sananiri's cell.

My connection with Afghanistan began in the summer of 1980 by a twist of fate, when I was temporarily filling in for one of my colleagues at Al-Sayyidah Zaynab Clinic, which was administered by the Muslim Brotherhood's Islamic Medical Society.

One night the clinic director, a Muslim Brother, asked me if I would like to travel to Pakistan to contribute, through my work as a surgeon, to the medical relief effort among the Afghan refugees. I immediately agreed because I saw this as an opportunity to get to know one of the arenas of jihad that might be a tributary and a base for jihad in Egypt and the Arab region, the heart of the Islamic world, where the basic battle of Islam was being fought.

The problem of finding a secure base for jihad activity in Egypt used to occupy me a lot, in view of the pursuits to which we were subjected by the security forces and because of Egypt's flat terrain which made government control easy, for the River Nile runs in its narrow valley between two deserts that have no vegetation or water. Such a terrain made guerrilla warfare in Egypt impossible and, as a result, forced the inhabitants of this valley to submit to the central government and be exploited as workers and compelled them to be recruited in its army.

The outlet for pent-up resentment was the explosions that occurred at infrequent intervals just like an extinct volcano that no one knows when it will erupt, or like an earthquake that no one knows when it will shake the ground with all that lies on it. It was not strange, therefore, that the history of the contemporary Islamist movement since the 1940s has been one of repeated crackdowns by the authorities."

For this reason this invitation (to participate in medical assistance to the Afghan refugees) came as a predestined event. I accepted the invitation out of an earnest wish to get to know the suitable arenas where I could establish a secure base for jihadist action in Egypt, particularly during the term of Anwar al-Mujahideen when the signs of a new crusade became apparent to everyone who had perspicacity and was obvious to everyone concerned about his nation's affairs.

And so I actually left for Peshawar in Pakistan in the company of a colleague who was an anesthetist. We were soon followed by another colleague who specialized in plastic surgery. We were the first three Arabs to arrive there to participate in relief work among the Afghan refugees.

We were preceded to Peshawar by Kamal al-Sananiri, may he rest in peace.

We could see that he had left his mark wherever we went. He had played a pioneer role in establishing the hospital where we worked and whenever we met with mujahideen leaders, they would speak of his assistance to them and his efforts to unite them. Although I never met him, his actions and contributions demonstrated his generosity and beneficial services in the cause of God.

It was not strange that Al-Sananiri should be killed in the campaign of arrests that began with (Al-Mujahideen's) decision to take certain persons into custody in September 1981.

Kamal al-Sananiri was killed by acts of torture personally carried out by Hasan Abu-Basha, director of the State Security Investigation Department and later interior minister. One must pause and ponder the story of the killing of Kamal al-Sananiri (may he rest in peace).

Kamal al-Sananiri was arrested in September 1981 and after Anwar al-Mujahideen was assassinated in October of the same year, the regime realized that the State Security Investigation Department, military intelligence, and general intelligence were completely unaware of the pent-up resentment that seethed inside Egypt.

Indeed the State Security Investigation Department's ignorance about what was happening in Egypt made it reassure Al-

Mujahideen that its campaign of arrests against opposition figures in September 1981 had secured the country in his favor and protected him from political opposition in general, and Islamist opposition in particular.

For this reason the investigation department hastened to begin a new investigation of the Muslim Brotherhood despite its earlier conviction that the Muslim Brothers were peaceable. The investigation focused on persons in the second and third ranks of leadership. Prominent among these persons was Kamal al-Sananiri.

Several considerations were taken into account in making this choice including the fact that the Muslim Brotherhood's General Guide Umar al-Talmasani was an old man who could not tolerate torture, and his moral status as general guide would cause problems for the regime. The regime also knew that actual power and the details of the Muslim Brotherhood's activities were not in Umar al-Talmasani's hands, including the extensive activity carried out by Al-Sananiri in maintaining communication between the Muslim Brotherhood in Egypt and its international branch abroad.

Al-Sananiri used to travel a lot abroad for this purpose. He also sponsored the Afghan cause and was a pioneer in backing the Afghan jihad and maintaining contacts with its leaders. He also had a prominent status inside the Muslim Brotherhood.

The Muslim Brotherhood had a peculiar organizational structure. The overt leadership was represented by General Guide Umar al-Talmasani, who was the leader in the eyes of the population and the regime. Actually the real leadership was in the hands of the Special Order Group that included Mustafa Mashhur, Dr. Ahmad al-Malat, may he rest in peace, and Kamal al-Sananiri, may he rest in peace. This made the State Security Investigation Department believe that if the Muslim Brotherhood had another secret organization, its secrets would be known by Kamal al-Sananiri."

The interrogation of Kamal al-Sananiri began in a brutal manner. Dr. Abd-al-Mun'im Abu-al-Futuh, my colleague in my medical school days, once told me this story while we were talking across the windows of our cells in Al-Qal'ah jail.

He said that Kamal al-Sananiri was taken in front of his brothers, including Abu-al-Futuh, from his cell in the Turrah prison, which was used as a way station before prisoners were moved to other jails. He was dressed in a gellaba and a cloak.

Abd-al-Mun'im Abu-al-Futuh did not see him after that except at the headquarters of the Socialist Public Prosecutor. His body was swollen and the signs of severe torture were apparent on him. He told his colleagues that he was being subjected to a level of torture to which he had not been subjected during the era of (former President) Jamal Abd-al-Nasir. Al-Sananiri informed the interrogator who questioned him at the office of the Socialist Public Prosecutor that he had been tortured.

Sometime later one of the prison guards, a sergeant, told Abd-al-Mun'im Abu-al-Futuh, that one of their brothers had been killed under torture.

Abu-al-Futuh later found out that it was Al-Sananiri.

The Interior Ministry announced that he had committed suicide by hanging himself from a water pipe in his solitary cell with the belt of the dressing gown he was wearing after writing this sentence on the wall: "*I have killed myself to protect my brothers.*"

33

Another witness who was present at his torture told me that Kamal al-Sananiri, may he rest in peace, on the last night of his life was tortured with extreme severity.

The strange thing after all these well-known facts, of which the Muslim Brothers were well aware, is that they did not act to avenge his blood, although they knew all the details about the way he was killed. They did not even bring a lawsuit against those responsible for his death, whose identities were known, and it would have been easy to prove their responsibility in court. Kamal al-Sananiri entered jail on his feet and left it as a lifeless corpse. The prison warden, the prisons department, and the Interior Ministry were responsible for what happened and an autopsy would have refuted any story fabricated by the Interior Ministry to explain his death."

### Time in Peshawar

When I came into contact with the arena of Afghan jihad in 1980, I became aware of its rich potential and realized how much benefit it would bring to the Muslim nation in general, and the jihadist movement in particular. I understood the importance of benefiting from this arena. Hence, after I stayed for four months there on my first visit, I returned in

March 1981 and spent another two months there. I was then forced to return to Egypt because of pressing circumstances back home.

It was then God's will, may He be praised and Whom we thank for the good and the bad that befalls us, that I should spend three years in an Egyptian jail that ended in late 1984 but, because of certain private circumstances, I was unable to return to the arena of Afghan jihad until mid-1986.

During my contacts and dealings with those who worked in that arena, several vitally important facts became clear to me and it is necessary to mention them here:

1.     A jihadist movement needs an arena that would act like an incubator where its seeds would grow and where it can acquire practical experience in combat, politics, and organizational matters. The brother martyr-for this is how we think of him-Abu-Ubaydah al-Banshiri, may he rest in peace, used to say: 'It is as if 100 years have been added to my life in Afghanistan.'

2.     The Muslim youths in Afghanistan waged the war to liberate Muslim land under purely Islamic slogans, a very vital matter, for many of the liberation battles in our Muslim

world had used composite slogans, that mixed nationalism with Islam and, indeed, sometimes caused Islam to intermingle with leftist, communist slogans. This produced a schism in the thinking of the Muslim young men between their Islamic jihadist ideology that should rest on pure loyalty to God's religion, and its practical implementation.

The Palestine issue is the best example of these intermingled slogans and beliefs under the influence of the idea of allying oneself with the devil for the sake of liberating Palestine. They allied themselves with the devil, but lost Palestine.

Another important issue is the fact that these battles that were waged under non-Muslim banners or under mixed banners caused the dividing lines between friends and enemies to become blurred. The Muslim youths began to have doubts about who was the enemy. Was it the foreign enemy that occupied Muslim territory, or was it the domestic enemy that prohibited government by Islamic shari'ah, repressed the Muslims, and disseminated immorality under the slogans of progressiveness, liberty, nationalism, and liberation. This situation led the homeland to the brink of the abyss of domestic ruin and surrender to the foreign enemy, exactly like the current situation of the majority of our (Arab) countries under the aegis of the new world order.

## Fighting against the Russians

In Afghanistan the picture was completely clear: A Muslim nation carrying out jihad under the banner of Islam, versus a foreign enemy that was an infidel aggressor backed by a corrupt, apostatic regime at home. In the case of this war, the application of theory to the facts was manifestly clear. This clarity was also beneficial in refuting the ambiguities raised by many people professing to carry out Islamist work but who escaped from the arena of jihad on the pretext that there was no arena in which the distinction between Muslims and their enemies was obvious.

3.     Furthermore, the Afghan arena, especially after the Russians withdrew, became a practical example of jihad against the renegade rulers who allied themselves with the foreign enemies of Islam. Najibullah in Afghanistan was an example that we had seen before. He prayed, fasted, and performed pilgrimage. At the same time he prohibited government by Islam and allied himself with the enemies of Islam, allowed them to enter his

country, and brutally oppressed the Muslims and the mujahideen.

4.      A further significant point was that the jihad battles in Afghanistan destroyed the myth of a (superpower) in the minds of the Muslim mujahideen young men. The USSR, a superpower with the largest land army in the world, was destroyed and the remnants of its troops fled Afghanistan before the eyes of the Muslim youths and as a result of their actions.

That jihad was a training course of the utmost importance to prepare Muslim mujahideen to wage their awaited battle against the superpower that now has sole dominance over the globe, namely, the United States.

It also gave young Muslim mujahideen-Arabs, Pakistanis, Turks, and Muslims from Central and East Asia-a great opportunity to get acquainted with each other on the land of Afghan jihad through their comradeship-at-arms against the enemies of Islam.

In this way the mujahideen young men and the jihadist movements came to know each other closely, exchanged expertise, and learned to understand their brethren's problems."

While the United States backed Pakistan and the mujahideen factions with money and equipment, the young Arab mujahideen's relationship with the United States was totally different.

Indeed the presence of those young Arab Afghans in Afghanistan and their increasing numbers represented a failure of US policy and new proof of the famous US political stupidity. The financing of the activities of the Arab mujahideen in Afghanistan came from aid sent to Afghanistan by popular organizations. It was substantial aid.

The Arab mujahideen did not confine themselves to financing their own jihad but also carried Muslim donations to the Afghan mujahideen themselves. Usama Bin Ladin has apprised me of the size of the popular Arab support for the Afghan mujahideen that amounted, according to his sources, to $200 million in the form of military aid alone in 10 years.

Imagine how much aid was sent by popular Arab organizations in the non-military fields such as medicine and health, education and vocational training, food, and social assistance (including sponsorship of orphans, widows, and the war handicapped. Add to all this the donations that were sent on special occasions such as Eid al-Fitr and Eid al-Adha feasts and during the month of Ramadan.

Through this unofficial popular support, the Arab mujahideen established training centers and centers for the call to the faith. They formed fronts that trained and equipped thousands of Arab mujahideen and provided them with living expenses, housing, travel, and organization.

### Changing Bin Ladin's Guard

About the Afghan Arabs' relationship with the United States, Al-Zawahiri says in his book: "If the Arab mujahideen are mercenaries of the United States who rebelled against it as it alleges, why is it unable to buy them back now? Are they not counted now-with Usama Bin Ladin at their head-as the primary threat to US interests? Is not buying them more economical and less costly that the astronomical budgets that the United States is allotting for security and defense?

"The Americans, in their usual custom of exaggeration and superficiality, are trying to sell off illusions to the people and are ignoring the most basic facts. Is it possible that Usama Bin Ladin who, in his lectures in the year 1987, called for boycotting US goods as a form of support for the intifadah in Palestine, a US agent in Afghanistan?

I remember that he visited us in those days at the Kuwaiti-funded Al-Hilal Hospital in Peshawar and talked to us about those lectures of his. I remember that I told him: 'As of now, you should change the way in which you are guarded. You should alter you entire security system because your head is now wanted by the Americans and the Jews, not only by the communists and the Russians, because you are hitting the snake on its head.

Furthermore, is it possible that the martyr-as we regard him-Abdallah Azzam was a US collaborator when in fact he never stopped inciting young men against the United States and used to back HAMAS with all the resources at his disposal?

Is it possible that the jihadist movement in Egypt can be a collaborator movement for the United States when Khalid al-Islambuli and his comrades killed Anwar al-Mujahideen, even before the phenomenon of the Arab mujahideen in Afghanistan emerged?

Is it possible that the jihadist movement in Egypt can be a US collaborator movement when in fact it brought up its children, ever since the movement started, to reject Israel and all the agreements of capitulation to it and to consider making peace with Israel as a contravention of Islamic Shari'ah?

The United States was taken aback by the fact that its scheme in Afghanistan was spoiled by the "Arab Afghans" and by the Afghan mujahideen themselves who had true hearts.

The United States wanted the war to be a war by proxy against the Russians, but, with God's assistance, the Arab mujahideen turned it into a call to revive the neglected religious duty, namely jihad for the cause of God.

For this reason the United States was alert to this danger in Bosnia-Herzegovina. Its primary condition to implement the Dayton agreement was to expel all the Arab mujahideen from Bosnia-Herzegovina.

The seriousness of the presence of Muslim, particularly Arab, young men in the arena of Jihad in Afghanistan consisted of turning the Afghan cause from a local, regional issue into a global Islamic issue in which the entire nation can participate.

## Why We Blew Up the Egyptian Embassy in Pakistan?

After the campaign to expel the Arab mujahideen from Pakistan began, the Egyptian Government began to act like a lion in Pakistan, relying on the backing given to it by the United States, which has strong influence on the Pakistani Government.

Earlier-since the 1950s--the Egyptian Government's relationship with the Pakistani Government had been bad because the Egyptian Government used to back India on the Kashmir issue. Ever since the days of Jamal Abd-al-Nasir, the Egyptian Government regarded Kashmir as a domestic Indian problem.

The Egyptian Government began to pursue the Arabs, but particularly Egyptian nationals, who had stayed on in Pakistan. The situation got the point where a student at Islamabad's Islamic University who was residing legally in the country was deported.

Furthermore two Egyptians who had acquired Pakistani citizenship because they had married Pakistani women were arrested. The Pakistani Government's attitude of surrender got to the point where it handed over these two naturalized Pakistanis to the Egyptian Government before the Pakistani courts could finish examining their petition, with total disregard for Pakistani law and the Pakistani constitution.

The expansion of the Egyptian Government's anti-fundamentalist campaign in Egypt and the fact that it transferred the battle to areas outside Egypt required a response.

For this reason we decided that our response should be an attack on a target that would hurt this vile alliance. After some consideration, we decided to form a team that would carry out the response. It was instructed to hit the following targets:

First: To hit the US Embassy in Pakistan, and if not possible, to hit another US target in the country, and again if not possible to attack the embassy of a Western country famous for its historical enmity to the Muslims, and if not possible, to hit the Egyptian Embassy.

After extensive surveillance, it was decided that hitting the US Embassy was beyond the team's capability. Surveillance was conducted on another US target in Islamabad but it was discovered that it had a very small number of

US personnel and that most of the casualties would be among Pakistani nationals.

It was also discovered that hitting the other Western embassy was beyond the team's capabilities. Hence, it was finally decided to hit the Egyptian Embassy in Islamabad, which was not merely conducting the pursuit campaign against the Arab Afghans in Pakistan but was also playing a serious espionage role against the Arab Afghans. Later the Pakistani security agencies discovered among the debris of the ruined embassy documents that revealed Indian-Egyptian cooperation in the field of espionage.

Prior to the attack, the team entrusted with the bombing sent us word saying that it could hit both the US and Egyptian embassies if we could come up with an additional sum of money. We had provided what we could, however, and could not provide any more. Hence the team focused on blowing up the Egyptian Embassy. It left the embassy's ruined building as an eloquent and clear message.

### Jihad Movement in Egypt

The jihad movement in Egypt began its current march against the government in the mid-1960s when the Nasirite regime began its famous campaign against the Muslim Brotherhood (MB) group in 1965. Some 17,000 members of the Muslim Brotherhood were put in prison and Sayyid Qutub (one of the most prominent MB thinkers) and two of his comrades were executed. The authorities thought that they had eradicated the Islamic movement in Egypt once and for all.

But God willed that those events were the spark that ignited the jihad movement in Egypt against the government.

The Islamic movement in Egypt, even though it made an effort (marasat al-juhd) against the enemies of Islam in the past, its general line was not against the ruling regime but against the external enemy. The movement's ideology and media continued to try to get close to the head of the ruling regime (the king) and to recognize him as the legitimate authority in the country.

This arbitrary separation between the external enemies and their internal agents led to many disasters and setbacks because the movement's members faced their enemy with their chests but left their backs exposed to his ally. Thus, they were stabbed in the back on the orders of those whom they faced with their chests.

## Sayyid Qutub

(Sayyid Qutub) affirmed that the issue of unification in Islam is important and that the battle between Islam and its enemies is primarily an ideological one over the issue of unification. It is also a battle over to whom authority and power should belong-- to God's course and shari'ah, to man-made laws and material principles, or to those who claim to be intermediaries between the Creator and mankind.

This affirmation greatly helped the Islamic movement to know and define its enemies. It also helped it to realize that the internal enemy was not less dangerous than the external enemy was and that the internal enemy was a tool used by the external enemy and a screen behind which it hid to launch its war on Islam.

The group rallying around Sayyid Qutub decided to deal blows to the existing government in its capacity as a regime that was hostile to Islam and which departed from the course of God and refused to apply the shari'ah.

The group's plan was simple. It did not aim to overthrow the regime or to create a vacuum of power but to deal to the regime preventive, defensive, and retaliatory blows if it planned a new campaign of repression against Muslims.

However, the meaning of this plan was more important than its material strength. The meaning was that the Islamic movement had begun a war against the regime in its capacity as an enemy of Islam. Before that, the Islamic movement's ethics and principles--and in which some believe until now--affirmed that the external enemy was the only enemy of Islam.

Although the Nasirite regime tortured and maltreated Sayyid Qutub's group, it failed to stop the growing influence of this group among Muslim youth.

Sayyid Qutub's call for loyalty to God's oneness and to acknowledge God's sole authority and sovereignty was the spark that ignited the Islamic revolution against the enemies of Islam at home and abroad. The bloody chapters of this revolution continue to unfold day after day.

The ideology of this revolution and the clarity of its course are getting firmer every day. They are strengthening the realization of the nature of the struggle and the problems on the road ahead--the road of the prophets and messengers and their followers until God Almighty inherits the earth and those who live on it.

Professor Sayyid Qutub played a key role in directing the Muslim youth to this road in the second half of the 20th century in Egypt in particular and the Arab region in general."

After the execution of Sayyid Qutub his words acquired dimensions not acquired by any other religious scholar. Those words, which Qutub wrote (metaphorically) with his own blood, became the landmarks of a glorious and long road and the Muslim youth came to realize how much the Nasirite regime and its communist allies panicked from Sayyid Qutub's call for unification.

Sayyid Qutub became an example of sincerity and adherence to justice. He spoke justice in the face of the tyrant (Jamal Abd-al-Nasir) and paid his life as a price for this. The value of his words increased when he refused to ask for pardon from Jamal Abd-al-Nasir. He said his famous words, "the index finger (which holds the prayer beads) that testifies to the oneness of God in every prayer refuses to request a pardon from a tyrant.

The Nasirite regime thought that the Islamic movement received a deadly blow with the execution of Sayyid Qutub and his comrades and the arrest of thousands of Islamic movement members. But the apparent calm on the surface concealed under it an immediate interaction with Sayyid Qutub's ideas and calls and the beginning of the formation of the nucleus of the modern Islamic jihad movement in Egypt.

Thus this nucleus, which the writer of this book joined, was formed in the shape of the Al-Jihad Organization. Events added another serious factor that affected the march of the jihad movement in Egypt, namely, the 1967 setback. The symbol Jamal Abd-al-Nasir--whose followers tried to depict to the people as the immortal and invincible leader--fell.

The tyrant leader, who mistreated his foes and threatened them in his speeches, became a man panting after a face-saving peaceful solution.

The jihad movement realized that the woodworm had begun to eat the idol until he became weak because of the effects of the setback and he fell to the ground amid the bewilderment of his priests and the horror of his worshippers. The jihad movement became more resolved, realizing that its archenemy was an idol created by a huge propaganda machine and a campaign of repression against defenseless and innocent people.

The Nasirite regime then received a deadly blow represented by the death of Jamal Abd-al-Nasir three years after the setback, three years that he lived suffering from the consequences of the defeat. Thus, the myth of the Leader of Arab nationalism who would throw Israel into the sea was destroyed.

The death of Abd-al-Nasir was not the death of one person but also the death of his principles, which proved their failure on the ground of reality, and the death of a popular myth that was broken on the sands of Sinai.

The huge funeral held for Abd-al-Nasir was only the residue of the state of unconsciousness that prevailed among the Egyptian masses thanks to his strong media and a kind of farewell by the Egyptians to their ruler. Soon they replaced him with another ruler, who took another turn and started to sell them a new illusion.

A few years later, the name of Jamal Abd-al-Nasir would only arouse feelings of indifference among ordinary Egyptians.

Al-Mujahideen took the fundamentalists out of the bottle

Anwar al-Mujahideen's assumption of power marked the beginning of a new political transformation in Egypt represented by the end of the Russian era and the start of the American era. Like every transformation, this transformation started shaky and weak but it gradually became stronger and its features began to become clearer with the passage of time.

Al-Mujahideen began removing the proteges of the old regime. His strongest weapon in resisting those remaining proteges was his permission of some forms of freedom for the repressed people.

As soon as some pressure was lifted from the Islamic movement, the giant (the Islamic movement) emerged from the bottle and the extensive influence of the Islamists among the masses became clear. Muslim youth won the overwhelming majority of the seats in university and school student unions in a matter of few years. The Islamic movement began its march to control the trade unions.

A new phase of growth began for the Islamic movement. But this time there was no repetition of the past; rather the Islamic movement built on it, benefiting from previous experiences, lessons, and events.

The Islamic movement began entering this phase of growth, spreading among its youth a deep awareness that that the internal enemy was not less dangerous than the external enemy. This awareness began to strongly grow on the basis of clear legitimacy and bitter historical and practical experience.

Some old symbols tried and are still trying to reiterate worn-out concepts that fighting can only be against the external enemy and that there is no collision between Islamic movements and their governments. However, the new awareness was stronger in its legal bases and clearer in its practical experience of all these illusions

### The Military Technical College affair

The military technical college group began to be formed after the arrival of Salih Siriyah in Egypt where he started to make contacts with Muslim Brotherhood symbols, such Mrs. Zaynab al-Ghazali and Hasan al-Hudaybi, and to form a group of young people, urging them to confront the ruling regime.

Salih Sariyah was a mesmerizing speaker and a highly intellectual person, who received a doctorate in education from Ain Shams University (in Cairo). He knew very well shari'ah science. I met Sariyah once during an Islamic jamboree at the College of Medicine. Sariyah had been invited to the jamboree to deliver a speech.

As soon as I heard the speech by this visitor I realized that his words carried weight and meaning on the need to support Islam. I decided to meet this visitor but all my attempts were in vain.

The group formed by Sariyah grew and was able to recruit a number of Military Technical College students, including Karim al-Anadoli.

The youth began putting pressure on Sariyah to start the confrontation. Under their pressure he agreed to carry out an attempt to overthrow the regime. A plan was prepared under which group members would silently overpower the policemen guarding the college gate, enter the college, and seize weapons and armored vehicles with the help of students acting as night supervisors. They would then march toward the Arab Socialist Union headquarters to attack Al-Mujahideen and his government officials who were meeting there.

The coup attempt failed because it did not take into consideration the objective conditions and the need to prepare well for it. The group who attacked the gate was untrained. The plan also met other difficulties during implementation.

But the meaning that I would like to stress is that the Islamic movement after Abd-al-Nasir successive blows to it proved that it was too big to be eradicated and too strong to be pushed into despair and frustration. This movement spawned a new generation a few years after the 1967 defeat. This generation returned to the field of jihad, brandishing its weapon against ruling regime, which was hostile to Islam and which was allied with the United States this time.

This operation (coup attempt) proved that the young mujahideen did not differentiate between the old Nasirite-Russian era and the new Al-Mujahideen era; both eras were equally hostile (to Islam).

### Salih Sariyah

Although this operation was nipped in the bud, it marked the new change in the general march of the Islamic movement, which decided to carry arms against the government. Earlier (during Abd-al-Nasir era) the Islamic movement carried arms against the Nasirite repression campaign to prove that repression did not work and that what Abd-al-Nasir's cronies thought was a campaign to rout out the jihadi current in 1965 was just the spark that revived the movement.

The group was taken to court and Salih Sariyah, Karim al-Anadoli, and Talal al-Ansari were sentenced to death.

The government started to haggle with the three to submit a pardon request to the president of the republic. Karim al-Anadoli submitted a pardon request as a result of which his death sentence was commuted to life imprisonment. Salih Sariyah and Talal al-Ansari refused to submit a pardon request.

One day, political prisoners gathered around Salih Sariyah in the prison's small courtyard and urged him to submit a pardon request. He told them: What power does Al-Mujahideen have to prolong my life? He then told them: Look at this gloomy prison, this bad food, and these blocked lavatories in which we throw this food. This is the real life. Why should we cling to it?

During the last visit before execution day Salih Sariyah's wife came with her nine children to the prison. He told her: If you submit a pardon request, you are divorced.

On execution day, a force from the prison and the state security investigation department entered the cell of Talal al-Ansari to tie him and take him to the scaffold. He asked them to let him pray and kneel twice. The state security investigating department officer told him: Pray when you go to whom you are going.

Two prisoners--Adil Faris and Salih Faris-- heavily beat that officer and gouged one of his eyes out. The officer then left work at the state security investigation department. As for Adil and Salih Faris, they emigrated from Egypt. Adil Faris went to Afghanistan where he was killed in the Nahrin battle in northern Afghanistan.

### Revival of the al-Jihad Organization

After several years those who left prison from the Technical Military College case tried to revive the organization twice. The first attempt ended with the arrest of the group in 1977. The second attempt ended with the arrest of the group in 1979 because of the presence of an undercover agent among them.

Muhammad Abd-al-Salam Faraj, author of the book the "Absent Duty" (Al-Daribah al-Gha'ibah), was among those arrested in the second group. Faraj's activity was concentrated in Cairo, Giza, and northern Egypt.

At the same time, the Salafi jihadi current was controlling university student unions in southern Egypt and rejecting the Muslim Brotherhood's attempts to contain it and make it join the line of pacification with the government.

Those youth in southern Egypt universities began to know Shaykh Omar Abdel Rahman and to invite him to their lectures, conferences, and jamborees.

After controlling the universities these youth moved to work among the masses outside the universities. Their most important activities were noisy demonstrations and meetings against peace with Israel and Al-Mujahideen's hosting of the Shah of Iran in Egypt.

Muhammad Abd-al-Salam Faraj and his comrades met with the youth in southern Egypt. With the unification of these two currents the Islamic Group (Al-Jama'ah al-Islamiyah) was formed under the leadership of Omar Abdel Rahman, who is now serving a life sentence in Rochester prison in Minnesota in the United States on charges of involvement in the (1993) New York bombings.

## The Assassination of Anwar Al-Mujahideen (President Anwar al Sadat)

> *Among the Believers men who have been true to their Covenant with God: Of them some have completed their vow (to the extreme), and some (still) wait: But they have never changed (their determination) in the least. (Qu'ran)*

The Assassination of Al-Mujahideen was part of a plan to kill the upper echelons of the regime and control the Radio Building and Asyut

The events of the rebellion of Dhu-al-Hujjah 1401 Anno Hegira, corresponding to October 1981 AD, focused on two fronts:

The first front was the attack on Al-Mujahideen and the upper echelons of his regime during the military parade on 6 October and the attempt to kill the largest number of officials and seize the radio building (in Cairo). Activity on this front succeeded in killing Anwar al-Mujahideen but the upper echelons of the regime escaped and the attempt to seize the radio did not succeed.

The second front was the armed uprising in Asyut and the attempt to seize the city. The uprising started two days after the assassination of Al-Mujahideen; in other words, after the army succeeded in controlling the country and securing the regime. This attempt succeeded in seizing some police centers.

But the government summoned the Special Forces, which started pounding the resistance positions of the brotherly young mujahidin who were forced to leave these centers after running out of ammunition.

The armed rebellion in Asyut was doomed to fail. It was an 'emotional' uprising that was poorly planned. The rebellion occurred two days after the assassination of Al-Mujahideen and was based on an unrealistic plan to seize Asyut and then advance northward toward Cairo, disregarding any figures about the enemy's strength and material.

Thus the 1401 Hegira (1981) uprising ended with a fundamental gain--the killing of Al-Mujahideen. The attempts that followed it were not successful because of poor planning and insufficient preparation.

However, the issue must not be viewed from the angle of these small events. That uprising must be viewed from the angle of the aftereffects of these events and the facts that they proved. It is obvious that the uprising proved several facts:

1.  The events showed the courage of the fundamentalists who attacked forces that were more experienced and larger in number and equipment.

2.  The events showed the offensive nature of the fundamentalist movement, which decided to attack the regime in an attempt to kill its upper echelons among a huge crowd of spectators.

3.  The events showed that changing the regime, which had departed from Islam, became the central idea that preoccupied the Islamists, who rejected partial reform programs, patch-up jobs, and the attempts to beautify the ugly face of the regime with some reformatory measures.

4.  The events proved that the phase of the unilateralism of the regime in attacking the Islamic movement had ended and that the enemies of Islam in the White House and Tel Aviv and their agents in Cairo must expect a violent response to every repression campaign they carried out.

5.  The events proved that the idea of work through martial laws, submission to the secular constitution imposed by referendums, and recognition of the legitimacy of the government had become worn-out ideas in the minds of the Islamists. Those Islamists decided to carry arms to defend the absented creed, the banned shari'ah, their violated honor, their homeland that was occupied by new international imperialism, and their sanctities which were sold in the agreements of surrender with Israel.

6.  The events also showed the utter failure of the security services, which did not know that the country was charged with the jihadi current. This current was able to infiltrate the armed forces and to take from them some weapons and was able to join the military parade forces,

despite the tight security measures that were adopted to secure the parade.

I say that the youth of the 1981 uprising were 'pure' and vigilant, avoiding and even rejecting blandishments. They carried arms in defense of their religion, creed, sanctities, nation, and homeland.

## Egyptian acting prosecutor resorts to guerilla warfare

The technical military college operation was not the only one at that time. A few months after the operation Yahya Hashim made an attempt to start a guerilla war in the Al-Minya Mountains. Although this attempt did not succeed because it did not take into consideration the necessary objective conditions for the success of this kind of warfare, it was another indication that the change in the ideology of the Islamic movement had become a tangible fact. This fact indicated that the Muslim youth this time were no longer like their predecessors in the 1940s.

Yahya Hashim was a pioneer of jihad in Egypt. He was entitled to this title. God endowed him with a proud spirit and high morale, which prompted him to sacrifice everything, disregarding the vanities of this world. He had another good quality--his enthusiasm for what he believed in. He had--may God have mercy on him--a pure soul that sympathized with his brother Muslims.

Yahya Hashim was acting prosecutor--a post desired by many young men. But he did not care about this post. He was always ready to sacrifice this post for the sake of God, disregarding the ephemeral things of this world.

I got acquainted with Yahya Hashim and his nascent group after the June 1967 setback.

How he joined us was a unique story. At that time the country was sweeping with demonstrations, especially by university students and workers, protesting against the catastrophe suffered by the Nasirite regime and represented by the retreat of its forces before the Israeli forces.

The strongest Arab army--which the leader of the Arab nation (Jamal Abd-al-Nasir) had prepared to throw Israel and those behind Israel into the sea--was defeated. This huge army became remnants searching for escape in the Sinai desert from the Israeli Defense Forces

(IDF). The Air Force was destroyed on the ground before it could take off.

## Demonstration by "Al-Jihad" from Al-Husayn Mosque

We decided to stage a demonstration from the Mosque of Imam Al-Husayn, may God be pleased with him, and to proceed to the Al-Azhar Street and then to the center of Cairo in solidarity with the university students and workers in the Hulwan industrial area.

We went to the Imam Al-Husayn Mosque during the Friday prayer. We distributed ourselves in the corners of the mosque. After the prayer, Yahya Hashim stood up and addressed the people, explaining the setbacks suffered by the Muslim nation. We responded with shouts of "Allah Akbar."

But the detectives were prepared for this tense atmosphere. Undercover agents surrounded him and started pushing him outside the mosque with the people surprised by his dare which they were not used to during the Abd-al-Nasir era.

But Yahya did not stop shouting with a loud voice while the undercover agents surrounded him from all sides and pushed him outside.

When he was in the square outside the mosque, he continued to deliver his speech.

The undercover agents resorted to a trick to silence him. One of them seized him in the neck and told him: 'You thief, you have stolen my wallet.' The undercover agent started shouting with a voice louder than Yahya. Undercover agents gathered around him and pushed him into a nearby pharmacy, which they closed. Soon afterward a car came and took him to Hasan Tal'at, the director of the General Investigation Department (GID), at that time.

The Nasirite regime was confused and weak at that time. Its security services did not know how to react. They were between the two fires--a rotten and corrupt leadership paralyzed by the scandal of the defeat and a popular resistance that broke the barrier of fear and surprised these services with a new and unprecedented phenomenon of resistance and rejection. In the GID building, they beat him heavily and then took him to GID Director Hasan Tal'at.

Yahya Hashim told us about the interview that took place at Hasan Tal'at's office and the dilemma in which the regime had found itself. Popular anger had reached the judiciary ranks.

The GID director found himself before an acting prosecutor (Yahya Hashim) who enjoyed judicial immunity. The country was boiling like a volcano, which prevented the GID director from resorting to his usual methods of interrogation, especially of Muslims.

Hasan Tal'at started defending himself before Yahya Hashim, reiterating that he was a Muslim defending Islam while in fact he was promoted to that post because he served the regime at the expense of the blood and corpses of Muslims. But Yahya Hashim attacked him like a lion, refuting his claims. On the wall behind Hasan Tal'at's office was a frame with the name of God inside it. Yahya shouted him: 'Why do you put that frame over head while you do not know God?'

The regime was forced to retreat under those difficult conditions and it released Yahya Hashim willy-nilly.

The Imam Al-Husayn Mosque demonstration was an emotional outburst commensurate with our age then.

Yahyah Hashim did not leave an opportunity without inciting against the regime and calling for Jihad by Muslims. His activity coincided with the death of Abd-al-Nasir and the gradual release of Muslim Brotherhood members from prison at the beginning of the era of Al-Mujahideen.

Yahya Hashim met with several Muslim Brotherhood leaders. Due to his pure nature and strong emotion, he enthusiastically approached them as the legitimate leaders of the Islamic movement, as they had persuaded him.

He came to us carrying their visualization of work. Their visualization was that the leadership would be for them but that they would not be responsible for any problem occurring to any group. I told Yahya: 'This is an opportunistic attitude. They want the good things but not the bad things from leadership.'

But Yahya Hashim was unstoppable in his love for and trust of the Muslim Brotherhood.

However, God destined that he should discover the truth from a true experience. One of his brothers (comrades) had a security problem, which led him to hide from the security services. Yahya went to the Muslim Brotherhood leaders to help him solve the problem but he was shocked by their answer.

They told him that he must abandon this brother completely and not to give him any help. This shocked Yahya and led to an estrangement between him and the Muslim Brotherhood. Yahyah continued to take care of his brother and until he took him to a safe place.

The Technical Military College incident took place in 1974. Yahya Hashim sympathized with the mutiny and closely followed its news. At that time he began thinking of starting an armed confrontation with the government. He started urging those close to him to wage a guerilla war. He broached the idea to me but I did not approve it at all. I told him that the terrain of the country was not good for this kind of warfare and I gave him a book about guerilla warfare.

However, the idea continued to dominate him and a number of his brothers. Yahya Hashim began contacting a number of brothers accused in the Technical Military College incident. He began preparing a plan for their escape, exploiting his post as deputy prosecutor.

The basic idea was to secure a false order transferring them from their prison to another prison and to let them escape during the transfer. However, undercover agents uncovered the plan when they seized a letter smuggled to the suspects in the dock from the court's hall. After the seizure of the letter, which detailed the plan, Yahya Hashim decided to escape and to start his private project of guerilla warfare.

Yahya Hashim and his comrades escaped to a mountainous region in the Al-Minya Province on the edge of the desert. They bought some weapons and took up positions there on the pretext that they were a military unit. But the mayor of a neighboring village became suspicious and informed the police, which attacked them and arrested them after they ran out of ammunition. Yahya Hashim tried to pounce on the unit's commander, who opened fired at Hashim, killing him. This is the story of Yahyah Hashim, who was really a pioneer in jihad and who sacrificed everything for the sake of his beliefs.

Any company owner can publish a paid advertisement demanding the cancellation of a law or an administrative decision. Any actor can criticize the laws pertaining to his profession.

Any writer--such as Faraj Fawdah (who was killed by Muslim fudamentalists)--can object to and ridicule the shari'ah rulings. Any journalist can lambaste the government and object to its rules, decisions, and laws.

The only one who cannot do this is the mosque preacher. This is because article 201 of the penal code says: 'No one in a house of worship--even if he is a man of religion and is delivering a religious sermon--can say something that opposes an administrative decision or an existing law or regulation. Anyone who does this faces imprisonment and is fined 500 pounds. If he resists, the fine and imprisonment are doubled.

Further, the only people who are not allowed to form trade unions--a right that is guaranteed even to belly dancers in Egypt--are the religious preachers and scholars.

With the killing of Anwar al-Mujahideen the issue of jihad in Egypt and the Arab world exploded and became a daily practice. Confrontation of the regime, which was against the shari'ah and allied with America and Israel, became a battle of continuous chapters that did not stop until today. On the contrary, jihad is increasing day after day, gathering more supporters and increasingly threatening its enemies in Washington and Tel Aviv.

The issues that were triggered by the killing of Al-Mujahideen and the events that followed became basic issues in the minds of the Muslim youth.

Thus the issues of the supremacy of the shari'ah, the apostasy of the regime from Islam, and the regime's collaboration with America and Israel, became givens. The Muslim youth fought for these issues after Muhammad Abd-al-Salam Faraj and his brothers exploded them. These issues also exploded after after Khalid al-Islambuli said when he was asked why he killed Al-Mujahideen: "because he did not rule in accordance with the shari'ah, because he concluded sulh (conciliation) with peace, and because he insulted the scholars of Islam."

The animosity to Israel and America in the hearts of Islamists is genuine and indivisible. It is an animosity that has provided the "al-Qaeda" and the epic of jihad in Afghanistan with a continuous flow of "Arab Afghans.

The killing of Anwar al-Mujahideen at the hands of Al-Islambuli and his honorable comrades was a strong blow to the US-Israeli plan for the region. This proves the lies that are reiterated by Arab secularism that several jihad movements, especially those that participated in the Afghan jihad, are the creation of the United States.

One is surprised by the capacity of secular writers to lie. Seeing the overwhelming support in the Muslim world for the Islamic jihad movements, which dealt painful blows to the United States, they invented this lie, forgetting that agent Anwar al-Mujahideen was killed at the hands of fundamentalists in 1981,i.e. at the beginning of the Afghan jihad. These muihajidin participated in the Afghan jihad afterward.

The government's response to these events was brutal in its intensity and method.

The treadmill of torture and repression turned at full speed, writing a bloody chapter in the history of the modern history of the Islamic movement in Egypt. The brutal treadmill of torture broke bones, stripped out skins, shocked nerves, and killed souls. Its methods were lowly. It detained women, committed sexual assaults, and called men feminine names, starved prisoners, gave them bad food, cut off water, and prevented visits to humiliate the detainees. The treadmill of torture this time was different from previous ones in two ways:

It turned and is still turning non-stop. It has devoured thousands of victims since the killing of Al-Mujahideen. The shari'ah committee of the Lawyers Association estimated the number of grievances submitted from 1981 to 1991 at 250,000.

One time the government released 5,000 repentant prisoners in a few days. How many are those who have not repented?

In fact, the number of detainees in Egyptian prisons is not less in any case than 60,000. There is no way to contact them or to know their conditions in view of the tight security imposed on them by the government.

The State Security Investigation Department (SSID) and Military Intelligence referred the defendants to civil and military prosecutors. The investigations by the prosecutors were another chapter in the farce. The prosecutors were leaking the minutes of the interrogation to the SSID investigators who would ask the defendants about their confessions, beat them, and then dictate to them what they should say.

But the State security prosecutors this time lost their confidence in the regime. They saw with their eyes the intensity of the struggle between the regime and its foes. Therefore, they were eager to ensure that their collusion with the SSID investigators would not include material evidence against them if the situation changed and the regime fell.

The military public prosecutor investigating the assassination of Anwar al-Mujahideen ignored his responsibility and did not go to the parade stand except one day after the incident, although the incident was within his full jurisdiction. The assassinated person was the supreme commander of the armed forces, the assailants were members of the armed forces, and the incident occurred on military ground. But he waited for the results following the earthquake that struck the regime and paralyzed it.

The military public prosecutor was waiting to see whom he would interrogate, whom he would accuse, and whom he would prosecute.

The funny thing was that Colonel Mushin al-Sarsawi, chief of the detention prison in Turrah at that time (he was an example of those riding the wave and seizing the opportunity) entered the four-floor prison which was full of political detainees and shouted at them: 'O brothers in struggle, O brothers in struggle. President Anwar has been assassinated.

The military prosecutor quickly referred the defendants to military court on the charge of assassinating Anwar al-Mujahideen. The military court was formed under the presidency of Maj. Gen. Muhammad Samir Fadil.

Another farce of involving the military secularism of the Egyptian Army in repressing its Muslim foes took place after the Egyptian Army forgot about Israel and directed its weapons at its people.

The military trial witnessed repeated confrontations between the Islamic movement and its jihad vanguard with all its good quality, purity and offering and military secularism with all its falsity, hypocrisy, and corruption.

Military secularism always claimed that it respected Islam. But this respect had only one meaning for it, namely, employing religious scholars to pour praise on it to justify its acts. Indeed, the military court based its judgment on a fatwa by Shaykh Jad-al-Haq, the mufti of Egypt and later on the Shaykh of Al-Azhar. It used his fatwa to massacre young fundamentalists.

## Isam al Qamari

One of the most important jihad groups uncovered by the security agencies was that of Isam al-Qamari.

The name of Isam al-Qamari deserves a pause. Al-Qamari was a unique individual who has not been given enough credit for his work and his jihad activity because the media and propaganda tools in our countries are in the hands of groups that do not favor the Islamists. Accordingly, the right of publishing is controlled by them, to the exclusion of the Islamists. In doing so, they are following the footsteps of the West, where Jews are in control of the media and the propaganda tools.

Isam al-Qamari was a serious man who, since early in his youth, had taken the issue of Islam seriously. He decided to join the Military College to change the ruling regime in Egypt. That was his conviction as he finished his secondary school education. He once told me, God have mercy on him, that he asked his father once after joining the Military College: Do you know why I joined the Military College? His father said no. Al-Qamari said: To carry out a military coup in Egypt. His father was shocked but he could do nothing. Isam had already been admitted to the Military College.

Isam al-Qamari's grades upon graduating from high school qualified him to join such colleges as the College of Medicine, Engineering, etc. It was, and still is, the people's habit to prefer a scientific college to a military college, but Isam defied the prevailing trend for a certain reason.

At the Military College, Isam al-Qamari met Muhammad Mustafa Ulaywah, brother of 'Ulwi Mustafa Ulaywah, one of the activists in the Al-Jihad Group at the time. The two brothers made Al-Qamari join our jihad group. Thus, Isam al-Qamari joined the list of mujahideen in Egypt. From that moment until his death, Al-Qamari never stopped his fruitful and serious contributions and dedication for the sake of this religion.

He was assisted in this noble endeavor by his refined character and ethics. Isam was a man in the full sense of the word. He was a noble person in the true since of the word. Most of his sufferings and sacrifices that he endured willingly and calmly were the result of his honorable character, nobility, and self-respect.

After graduating from the Military College, Isam al-Qamari joined the Armored Corps, which he loved and in which he excelled. He used to tell us that this Corps must be the Corps of Muslims since it teaches people how to win battles and deter the enemy.

Al-Qamari's outstanding performance in the Armored Corps was noticeable. Isam gave all his time to studying and understanding military affairs and acquiring field experience in practice. For him, this was an endeavor for the sake of God. It was not strange, therefore, that Isam excelled in all his training courses and was always the first in his class.

For this reason, when he was a major he was nominated to receive training in the United States to command a battalion. He was promised that upon his return he would be appointed a commander in the Republican Guard, a position that Isam looked forward to with interest.

The only thing that dissuaded him from attending this course was one of brothers, may God forgive him, who exaggerated things and told him that 1981 would be the year of change in Egypt. He also told him that he was capable of recruiting a large number of struggling youths in the jihad groups.

### Smuggling Weapons From the Army

Based on this exaggerated statement, Isam decided not to travel to the United States. Instead, he was nominated to attend the Staff College. He was one of the few officers in the Armored Corps at the rank of a major who was nominated to attend this college.

Since Isam was convinced that 1981 would be the year of change, he and the fellow officers whom he recruited strove to smuggle as many weapons and ammunition from the army as possible, and we stored these weapons.

During the transfer of the last quantity of weapons from my clinic to the warehouse, and the weapons were in a bag along with books and some military bulletins, the man carrying the bag was arrested. However, he managed to escape without the bag. Through the bulletins that were inside the bag as well as the maps on which the locations of tanks in Cairo were outlined, it was possible to trace the group of officers working with Isam al-Qamari. Isam sensed the danger before they reached him so he escaped. However, some of his officers were arrested.

Isam remained at large from February to October 1981. He was arrested following the assassination of Anwar al-Mujahideen. Throughout this time Isam was patient, as was his custom. He did not complain, moan, or blame anybody. Instead, he tried to make it easy for his colleagues, support them, and strengthen their resolve.

Isam did not stop his activity while he was at large. On the contrary, despite his enormous problems, the stress, and the pressure that he lived under every minute, he did not stop working or exerting efforts.

He surveyed a number of targets, sites of troops, and police headquarters. He made plans and conducted several experiments.

When Anwar al-Mujahideen was assassinated, Isam asked me to connect him to the group that carried out the assassination. I introduced him to Abbud al-Zumur. At this delicate moment, Isam al-Qamari discussed the situation with Abbud and tried to save what could be saved, but it was too late.

## Attacking the US Presidents During Mujahideen's Funeral

Isam thought about attempting to hit the funeral of Anwar al-Mujahideen, including the (former) Presidents of the United States and the leaders of Israel. He also thought about seizing some tanks and using them to hit a vital target or attack Mujahideen's funeral.

However, the resources available were short of his ambitions and it was too late. Our meetings with Abbud al Zumur ended with an advice to him to try to leave Egypt at this stage to continue the attacks at another stage.

However, Abbud turned down our advice because he had promised the brothers to continue the battle. In prison, he admitted to me that he had been convinced by our opinion, but his promise to the brothers compelled him to turn it down.

Isam had a theory about jihad action that he tried hard to find the means to implement, but destiny would not permit him.

This theory continues to represent a suitable practical option, if the requirements for it are available, including:

- The security measures taken by our regimes are such that the only way to confront them is to deploy an armed force with a considerable firepower and armor enough to enforce its control of the capital, wage battles, and remain steadfast for one or two weeks.

- The Islamic movement possesses thousands of youths who are racing toward martyrdom, but these youths are not trained and lack combat experience.

- The Islamic movement's infiltration of the Army will always be countered by purging operations. It is difficult for the Islamic movement to recruit a large number of officers in the Army without getting discovered, in view of the tight security measures within the ranks of the Armed Forces.

- Isam's idea was to train hundreds of Muslim youths on weapons and how to use and drive tanks, even if it was a preliminary training.

- Isam looked lightly upon the police forces, the Central Security Forces, and the forces affiliated with the Interior Ministry.

- Isam criticized the Muslim youths for being preoccupied by the police and attacks on the police and for failing to examine the military situation from an analytical and practical perspective based on data.

Isam had much confidence in the young Muslim trainees. He used to say: The police forces have the upper hand against us because our brothers are not trained. If we train them and give them some weapons, nobody could stand against them.

This theory continued to be the subject of long discussions between us before and in prison. Many of his expectations proved to be valid, I must say.

His plan was a daring plan based on careful reconnaissance and scientific analysis of the realistic information. It suited Isam's personality, which had the same elements: Bravery, military knowledge, and hard work. This theory involveed many details and various aspects, but I just talked about its pivotal idea in passing.

## Al Jammaliyah Battle

Abbud Al Zumur ended up in Jail. By torturing his companions, the investigators learned that he had met Isam al-Qamari and me. It was a big surprise: The fugitive officer who has been at large for eight months surfaced again. After intensive pursuits, I was arrested. An attack was conducted on the hideout of Isam al Qamari, at the Cairo neighborhood of Al Jammaliyah, where an interesting battle took place.

This battle occupied an important place in the history of the movement because of the serious facts that it demonstrated about the confrontation between the Islamists and government troops. It also proved the validity of Isam's theory and his farsightedness. We must pause here a little to explain the details of this battle.

This battle took place in the Manshiyat Nasir area in the Al-Jammaliyah neighborhood. It is a poor area where poor homes are stacked next to each other, divided by narrow alleys and paths. Isam was hiding in a turner's workshop built by Muhammad Abdal Rahman al Sharqawi, along with Ibrahim Salamah Iskandarani and Nabil Na'im, to serve as one of our bases.

Al Sharqawi received a 7-year prison sentenced in connection with Al-Mujahideen's case then a 15-year term in the case of Tala'i Al-Fath. He is still at the Al-Aqrab Prison in Egypt. This workshop was in a modest house consisting of a roofless hallway, with two rooms on the right and two rooms on the left and an iron door at the beginning of the hallway.

The workshop was located in a narrow alley with a dead end and surrounded by several houses, many of them one-storied.

When the Interior Ministry learned that Isam was hiding in this workshop it surrounded the entire area with police and the Central Security Forces. It used the counterterror battalion in the Central Security Forces, the best unit available, to attack the workshop. The battalion surrounded the workshop for several hours and occupied the roofs of nearby buildings, where they mounted their machine guns.

Before dawn, the police called our brothers through loudspeakers and told them that the workshop was under siege and that they ought to surrender. Immediately after that, the break-in unit, which is made up of the best Central Security officers wearing shields, began the attack by spraying the door with an endless hail of bullets and shouting to the brothers to surrender. The brothers were awakened by this frightening noise.

Isam and his companions were prepared for this eventuality. They had an electric wire fastened a few centimeters away from the iron door.

They had two old short machine guns, two revolvers, and a number of hand grenades in their possession.

When the break-in troops tried to storm their way into the gate they were jolted, and they immediately retreated in shock. Isam seized the opportunity and hurled a hand grenade over the door. It landed in the middle of the break-in team, killing or wounding the team members. The battalion officers and soldiers panicked when they heard the screams of the break-in team.

There was complete silence in the air. Isam and his companions climbed to the roof of the workshop and started hailing the neighboring rooftops with bullets from their two machine guns, which soon stopped working. But Isam and his companions did not stop. They rained the force with 10 hand grenades, nine of which exploded. The resistance by the force stopped, and here Isam realized that it had been weakened. The brothers emerged from the workshop. They found a soldier in front of them pointing his weapon at them. However, he turned his back on them. Brother Nabil Na'im shot him in the head.

Isam asked them to sit still and wait for him to
throw a hand grenade then start running in the
direction of the grenade. The brothers started
running through the cordons of the siege. It
was as if they were running amidst dead
people and ghosts. They continued to run until
they reached the neighboring hills of Al-
Muqattam. From a distance, they sat down to
watch the badly hurt troops as they gathered
their wounded men and moved back to their
vehicles. Ibrahim Salamah suggested that this
was the best opportunity to attack the battalion
with what was left with the brothers in terms
of ammunition, but Isam decided it was
enough

The brothers continued to walk on the hills of
Al-Muqattam. Ibrahim Salamah had a hand
grenade in his hand. He had removed the pin
from it then returned it again. However, it
seemed that the pin shifted out of place when
he was running. The brothers stopped for a
while near one of the caves.

Ibrahim Salamah wanted to urinate. He turned
around and faced the entrance of the cave.
Isam and Nabil sat a few meters away from
him with their backs to Ibrahim. The grenade
dropped on the floor, causing the pin to shift a
little. The brothers heard the capsule
exploding. Ibrahim immediately threw himself

on the bomb to protect his brothers. The silence of the night was broken by the explosion of the bomb, which ripped Ibrahim apart. He took the full power of the explosion.

It was an act of destiny that was beyond any expectation. After escaping safely from over a 100-man force from the Central Security Forces, Ibrahim met his fate. Isam and Nabil were astonished by the gravity of the surprise.

Isam was arrested and put on trial in the Al-Jihad case. The prosecutors, colluding with the intelligence department, did not take him to attend the first session of the trial. They brought him along with Rifa'I Taha (military official of the Islamic Group whom Damascus handed over to Egypt a few months ago) on the second session from their place of detention in Al-Qal'ah Prison.

Isam exposed this trick at the trial and insisted on explaining the harassment against him by the intelligence officers at the Al-Qal'ah Prison.

The judge tried to let it pass, but Isam insisted on continuing to talk. The judge threatened to kick Isam out of the courtroom, but Isam did not care. The judge ordered him out of the courtroom, but Isam refused. The Central Security Forces tried to carefully come closer to

Isam, but he shouted at them. They were scared and retreated.

Things went out of hand in the courtroom. The brother defendants were furious. As agreed with the brothers, I was in charge of things at the session. I asked the brothers to be quiet. I spoke in a loud voice and threatened that if Isam was kicked out of the courtroom by force--he was kept in a separate cage and isolated from the brother defendants--there would not be any trial. The atmosphere in the courtroom became tense. The judge realized that he was running an unprecedented case and that he risked a confrontation with the defendants. At this point the lawyers intervened to save the situation.

They apologized to the judge, amidst the deafening noise and shouts, so nobody really heard what they said. The judge seized the opportunity and said that the court had accepted the lawyers' apology. The trial was resumed.

### The Escape Plan from Turah Prison, the Cordons of Guards, and Crossing the River Nile

Throughout the prison period, Isam did not stop learning or teaching and educating members of the Al-Jihad group. All that he was thinking about was how to rescue the brothers, who were expected to receive the death penalty.

God Almighty willed that I had the honor of accompanying him for several months in the same cell in Turah Prison. Throughout that time he spent all his time thinking of scenarios about the future, finding practical solutions, and doing research into existing problems. We had to part. I was given a 3-year prison term, most of which I spent in prison before the verdict was issued. He received a 10-year prison term. As usual, he received the news with his unique calmness and self-composure. He even tried to comfort me and said: I pity you for the burdens that you will have to carry.

Isam remained in prison, and he continued to think of plans to escape. After several attempts, Isam, along with Khamis Musallam and Muhammad al-Aswani, managed to escape from the formidable Turah Prison on 17 July 1988. It was not an ordinary escape. It was preceded by long and complicated planning that was ultimately crowned with success. The escape involved a battle to cross the prison walls and go through the lines of guards watching the walls. It also involved crossing over to the other side of the Nile.

Without getting into details, the Interior Ministry was dumbfounded. It did not expect such a daring and noisy escape, which started with removing the bars of the cells, taking the warden guards prisoner, crossing the 4-meter high fence after throwing sound bombs, clashing with one of the guards and taking his weapon, and leaving the Turah Prison compound at midnight amidst the tight security.

After the escape of Isam al-Qamari and his colleagues from prison, they crossed the Nile to the other side and walked in the fields until they reached the central Delta.

Because they walked for such a long distance, Khamis Musallam's feet were injured and started to suppurate. He developed a fever and started to shiver. In an attempt to treat Khamis, the brothers resorted to Khalid Bakhit, a member of the Al Jihad Group, who gave them his house in the Al Sharrabiyah.

As fate would have it, a State Security Intelligence force came to the house of Khalid Bakhit early in the morning on July 25, 1988. It was part of the sweeping campaign of arrests that followed the escape of the three brothers.

Another courageous battle took place. As soon as the force commander, a Colonel in the State Security Intelligence Department, knocked on the door, he came under a hail of sound bombs that the brothers had prepared. Isam al-Qamari attacked him with a kitchen knife. The officer escaped, leaving his pistol behind. The other soldiers and officers retreated in fear. Isam picked up the pistol of the force commander and the brothers started running down to the street.

At the corner of the street, Isam al-Qamari engaged in a battle with the police force to cover his brothers' escape. He was hit in the stomach, and he fell. His companions returned to carry him, but he declined and gave them the pistol he had. He ordered them to continue to run away. He died on the spot.

This story, told by Nabil Na'im[1] demonstrates the frustration of the Interior Minister. Na'im told me that he had asked the officer at the Turah Prison jokingly after the escape: "Naturally, they will send you to Upper Egypt, right?"

---

[1] Nabil Na'im is a fundamentalist leader who is in prison in Egypt in connection with the Tala'i al-Fath al-Islami case,

The officer responded confidently: No; they will not do that. They should give me a medal for keeping Isam al-Qamari in prison all these years.

As it turned out, the officer was not removed from his post.

## Operations n Egypt

We could trace the start of the operations in Egypt as far back as Friday August 12, 1988, when the government carried out an aggression against the Ain Shams neighborhood in Cairo. After the sunset prayers, police troops stormed Adam Mosque, where the Islamic Group held its weekly seminar. It is worth noting that the police troops had raided the Adam Mosque several times before. Raiding mosques became a habit of the police forces, which destroyed everything inside them, tore down books, and fired tear gas and bullets indiscriminately.

The repeated aggressions against mosques until this very day will not pass unpunished, God willing. These crimes are the responsibility of the Interior Ministry and the US administration. These crimes are committed with the consent and before the eyes of this administration and in implementation of its policy of suppressing the Islamic resistance in favor of the Israeli expansion in the region.

The raid started with breaking the mosque's windows and firing tear gas and throwing incendiary bombs inside the mosque to force the people to leave. When the worshippers started to leave, the police forces stormed the mosque and opened fire indiscriminately.

This crime was enough to provoke the neighborhood residents, who spontaneously sided with the Islamic Group. As a result, the scope of disturbances expanded to include the entire area.

The Interior Ministry went mad and gave orders to open fire. Children, women, elderly, and youngsters fell victim. The streets and homes were full of wounded and dead people swimming in blood. Police trucks were full of detainees. It was natural for the people to respond. Two officers and four soldiers were wounded. Officer Muhammad Zakariya later died from wounds that he had sustained in the head.

Naturally, the Interior Ministry enforced a curfew in all streets in the area and sent large number of troops to the neighborhood.

The second campaign against Ain Shams neighborhood took place on Wednesday December 7, 1988, when Interior Ministry Zaki Badr received news about a peaceful march that the Islamic Group had intended to make toward the Al-Qubbah Presidential Palace to voice their support for the intifadah in occupied Palestine. The police would not allow the Islamic Group to express its opinion in the street through a demonstration, no matter what the reason for the demonstration was.

The police raided Adam Mosque before the dawn prayers and arrested those inside the mosque. It conducted a large-scale arrest campaign against all members of the Islamic Group in Ain Shams, Al-Matariyah, Alf Maskan, and Masakin Ain Shams. More than 180 people were arrested.

The government newspapers published a statement by the Interior Ministry admitting the campaign in Ain Shams and the detention of dozens of Islamic Group members. The statement claimed that leaflets and weapons had been seized with some of the detainees. The statement also admitted that the police forces had shut down Adam Mosque. The statement added that more combing operations would be conducted in search of the wanted Islamic Group members. The statement, however, failed to mention the detention of the mothers, wives, children, and relatives of the fugitive members as hostages to force them to give themselves up. It also failed to mention the brutal torture against the detainees to force them to identify the locations of their relatives.

## The Killing of Lieutenant Colonel Isam Shams, Deputy Chief of the Intelligence Unit

I remember well the killing of Lt. Col. Isam Shams, Deputy Chief of Eastern Cairo Intelligence Unit. In a rapid development, a peddler at Ain Shams marketplace stabbed police officer Lt. Col. Isam Shams, who died of his wounds. The peddler escaped. The investigations identified him as Sharif Muhammad Ahmad. He had been badly beaten several times by intelligence officers and arrested as part of the aforesaid August events, when he was tortured at Ain Shams police station.

The events ended with a bizarre theatrical performance in which Sharif Muhammad Ahmad, Khalid Isma'il, and Ashraf Darwish were shot dead.

A statement by the Interior Ministry claimed that the three had resisted the police forces that tried to arrest them for three hours in a street in Shubra, although not a single officer or soldier was hurt. The statement also claimed that weapons had been found next to the bodies of the three people. A leading figure of the Islamic Group in the area, called Jabir Muhammad Ahmad, was also killed and the police claimed that he had resisted the authorities and tried to kill an officer. The forces had to shoot him.

Following this incident, a curfew was imposed in the area and a massive campaign of arrests was conducted against suspects. One of the reasons behind this incident was the role of the aforesaid officer in the barbaric torture of detainees at Ain Shams Police Station.

Zaki Badr, who was Interior Minister at the time, ordered the arrest of 30 of the mothers, wives, and sisters of the fugitive leaders of the Islamic Group. After being brutally tortured at Ain Shams Police Station, they were transferred to the State Security Intelligence Department in Lazughli, where they were stripped of their cloths, slapped, kicked, and insulted.

The Ain Shams incidents represented a flagrant aggression against the Islamic Group and the entire inhabitants of the area. The purpose was clear; namely, to destroy the peaceful call activity undertaken by the Islamic Group in the area, which gained the support of the people, who were satisfied with the social and call activity carried out by the group members.

But the government, which adopted a policy of killing members of the Islamic Group and banning all their activities, would not allow this to continue. It was in implementation of the policy declared by Zaki Badr; namely, to hit hard where it hurts.

## An Ambush Against the Interior Minister's Convoy

The fundamentalist movement decided to respond to the Ain Shams incidents. The answer was to ambush Interior Minister Zaki Badr's motorcade using a booby-trapped car in December 1989. However, the ambush failed when the explosives in the car malfunctioned and its driver was arrested.

## The Killing of Alaa Muhi Al Din in the Street

The Interior Ministry responded to us by killing Dr. Alaa Muhi Al Din in broad daylight in the street on September 2, 1990. Muhi Al Din, may God bless his soul, was one of the leaders of the Islamic Group who advocated the dialogue with the government. He made this position known on several occasions. He raised the slogan of free dialogue, a policy that proved to be a total failure with our rulers.

Muhi Al Din's killing was a clear signal to the Islamic Group that the call for dialogue will be punished by death and that the regime will not tolerate the existence of the jihad groups. In doing so, the regime was doing the logical thing. The jihad groups represented the most serious opposition to it. They were the most capable of recruiting and spreading among the Muslim youths. These groups also represented a serious threat to the policy of normalization with Israel, which will not feel comfortable in Egypt so long as the threat of the Islamic groups existed.

The Islamic Group responded to the killing of Alaa Muhi Al Din by ambushing Interior Minister Abdel Halim Musa, but God willed that People's Assembly Speaker Rifaat al Mahjoub's motorcade happened to pass by the ambush, and he was killed.

Thus, the Islamic Group shifted its policy from long-term call activity to violence by fighting and resisting the government's aggression.

In the early 90s another important development took place. A large number of our brothers in the Al Jihad Group were arrested. More than 800 of them were put on trial in what came to be known as the Tala'i Al-

Fath cases. The court sentenced to death four of the defendants.

The government newspapers were elated about the arrest of 800 members of the Al Jihad Group without a single shot being fired. We decided to enter the battle of confrontation with the government, although our policy has always been to spread out and recruit elements in preparation for the battle of change.

Our response was to attack the convoy of Interior Minister Hasan al Alfi with a booby-trapped motorcycle. The Minister escaped death, but his arm was broken. A pile of files that he kept next to him saved his life from the shrapnel. This was followed by an attack carried out by the Islamic Group against Information Minister Safwat al Sharif, who survived the ambush.

This coincided with the Islamic Group's attack on the Commander of the Central Military Zone in his capacity as the commander who sanctioned all the verdicts issued by military courts. The attack failed because his car was bulletproof.

Let me discuss the death of innocent child Shayma. I deeply regret her death and and am willing to pay blood money. This girl was as old as my own daughter. Our brothers in the Al Jihad Group carried out the attack on the motorcade of Prime Minister Atif Sidqi using a booby-trapped car, but the Prime Minister survived the attack. His car escaped the full power of the explosion by a split second, although some shrapnel hit it.

As a result of the attack, a child named Shayma was killed. She was a student in a nearby school who was standing near the site of the incident.

The government used the death of Shayma, may God bless her soul, and portrayed the incident as an attack by the Al Jihad Group against Shayma, not against Prime Minister Sidqi.

Our brothers who carried out the attack had surveyed the area and noticed that there was a school under construction. They thought the school had no students in it. It transpired later that only the external part of the school was being renovated but the rest of the school was operating normally.

The unintended death of this innocent child pained us all, but we were helpless and we had to fight the government, which was against God's Shari'ah and supported God's enemies.

We had warned the people several times before that, particularly following the attack on Interior Minister Hasan al Alfi, to stay away from the pillars of the regime, their homes, and the routes they used. In their homes, offices, and motorcades, these officials are mixed with the public and they take cover behind them. So we have no choice but to hit them while cautioning the general public.

Our colleague Al Sayyid Salah summed this up by saying, when asked by investigators about the death of Shayma, that he regretted the killing of this child, but the jihad must not stop.

I explained this matter in detail in my letter entitled "Shifa Sudur al-Muslimim."

As regards the consequences resulting from the intentional harm done to Muslims, we have opted for the opinion of Imam al-Shafi'i, may God have mercy on him, who called for paying blood money to the relatives of those killed.

Therefore, we believe that those who kill Muslims unintentionally in such operations must pay blood money to their relatives.

If we want to put the issue of Shayma in perspective we must weigh her on one scale of the balance and put on the other scale our daughters and women who have lost their fathers and husbands for no reason other than that their fathers and husbands were performing the most honorable duty, the duty of jihad for the sake of God.

The regime dragged me, along with 280 others, to trial and the prosecution demanded the death sentence against us all. This meant that they wanted my daughter, who was two at the time, and the daughters of other colleagues, to be orphans. Who cried or cared for our daughters?

Police raided the home of Sayyid Qurani. When his daughter ran away in fear from the bullets, the police shot her dead immediately. Who shed tears for the daughter of Sayyid Qurani?

There are thousands of our women, sisters, and mothers who are standing at the doors of prisons in the hope of visiting their sons, brothers, and husbands. Who took interest in their tragedy?

The arm of Sana Abdel Rahman was broken when the police beat her brutally along with her 3-year daughter Khadijah in front of the Turah Prison. The mothers waiting in front of prison started to cry when one of the detainees told them, as he emerged from prison on his way to the court, that the detainees were dying. He added: Do anything. Go to the Prosecutor General. The Al-Sha'b newspaper published the photo of Sana with her arm in the cast and her daughter next to her.

Who is banning the hijab (veil) at schools and the niqab (face cover) at universities in order to fight the values of Islam and to force our daughters to emulate the west and its immorality?

Our colleagues in the Al-Jihad Group set up an ambush for Husni Mubarak's motorcade along the Salah Salim road, but he did not use that road on his way to perform the Eid prayers, so we failed.

There was another attempt to assassinate Husni Mubarak at Sidi Barrani Airport by members of the Islamic Group, but the attempt was discovered before we could carry it out.

As regards the most important operations carried out by fundamentalists from the Islamic Group, the killing of Maj. Gen. Ra'uf Khayrat on April 9, 1994 is one of the most important. Ra'uf Khayrat was one of the most dangerous officers in the State Security

Intelligence Department who fought the fundamentalists. He adopted several strict security precautions, such as changing his residence every few months, keeping his home unguarded, and driving his car personally to look like he was an ordinary person with no connection to the authority. However, the Islamic Group colleagues managed to reach him. As he was emerging from his home and about to get into his car, one of the brother mujahideen approached him and threw a bomb inside his car, and he was killed instantly.

The Islamic Group escalated the campaign and attacked the convoy of Husni Mubarak in Addis Ababa in the summer of 1995. The attack failed and Mubarak survived because one of the two cars that participated in the attack broke down.

Our colleagues in the Al Jihad Group planned two operations at almost the same time. The first was the bombing of the Egyptian Embassy in Islamabad in the autumn of 1995, and we talked about it in this book. The other operation was at home against Israeli tourists. It was known as the Khan al-Kkhalili case.

In July 1997 the Islamic Group inside prison announced its initiative to suspend violence unilaterally.

However, following this initiative a team from the Islamic Group carried out the Luxor operation against western tourists.

The above was a brief and quick summary of the most important acts of jihad between 1988 and 1997. Many details were skipped.

## Breaking the Will of the Fundamentalist Movement

Since the assassination of Anwar al Mujahideen, the campaign of repression aimed to break the will of the fundamentalist movement, particularly the fundamentalist groups. This policy took a serious escalatory turn when Zaki Badr took over the Interior Ministry. He declared that the remedy for the Islamic groups is to hit them deep in the heart.

It was clear that the purpose of the campaign was to instill despair in the hearts of the Muslim youths, lead them to believe that any resistance is futile and will only lead to disasters and calamities, and that surrender was the only choice.

Failure to respond to this campaign would have certainly led the Islamic movement to lose its self-confidence, retreat into silence and oblivion, and return to the terror of the Nasirite era. Driving people to despair of the worthiness of resistance has been the cornerstone of the policy of Jewish expansion in the region. Therefore, they realized that suppressing the resistance against them would not succeed unless they instilled despair in the hearts of the Muslims.

The response to this brutal campaign through jihad operation will not only protect the Muslim youths from despair but also fill their hearts with hope and self-confidence, after their trust in God Almighty.

The Muslim youths demonstrated that undermining the government and its henchmen was not difficult.

The fruits of the jihad resistance go beyond inspiring hope in the hearts of the Muslim youths. The resistance is a weapon directed against the regime's henchmen, who are demoralized as they see their colleagues falling around them. Furthermore, stepping up the jihad action to harm the US and Jewish interests creates a sense of resistance among the people, who consider the Jews and

Americans a horrible symbol of arrogance and tyranny.

Because of all this, there was no other choice but to continue the resistance. Any analyst could realize the extent of the disasters that could have taken place had Anwar al Mujahideen not been killed and had the resistance against the Egyptian Government stopped.

An analysis of the political situation in Egypt would reveal that Egypt is struggling between two powers: An official power and a popular power that has its roots deeply established in the ground, which is the Islamic movement in general and the solid jihad nucleus in particular.

The first power is supported by the United States, the west, Israel, and most of the Arab rulers. The second power depends on God alone then on its wide popularity and alliance with other jihad movements throughout the Islamic nation, from Chechnya in the north to Somalia in the south and from Eastern Turkestan in the east to Morocco in the west.

The reason for the enmity between the two forces is very clear. The first power insists on:

1. Removing Islam from power and keeping it away from the various aspects of life by force, brutality, and rigged elections.

2. Opening up the country to the enemies of Islam, the Americans and the Jews, through signing peace agreements and treaties that ban weapons of mass destruction for us only, disarming Sinai, and allowing direct US occupation of our land and holding joint military exercises.

It is a battle of ideologies, a struggle for survival, and a war with no truce.

After this brief and quick review of the history of the Islamic movement in Egypt we could pause here to examine the harvest of this recent past and era, which continued from 1966 until approximately 2000.

To answer this question, we could say that the harvest of this era could be summed up as follows:

1. Spreading: There is no doubt that the struggling Islamic movement has gained much ground during that period, particularly among the youths, and that it continues to grow and spread.

2. Collision: The Islamic movement has been on the offensive against the enemies of Islam. It demonstrated a sense of resistance until the last breath. The major events beginning with the incident at the Technical Military College in 1974 up to the Luxor incident in 1997 provide the best proof of this.

3. Continued dedication: The Islamic movement has offered tens of thousands of detainees and wounded and tortured people and thousands dead in its continuing struggle. This proved two things:

First; that its roots are strong and deeply established in the ground. Despite all these strikes and sacrifices, which no other political force in Egypt could have endured, this mujahid Islamic movement continues to operate for the sake of God.

Second; it continues to pose the main threat to the government's security. Proof of this is the continued existence of the emergency laws, military tribunals, and antiterror laws, which are not expected to be terminated anytime in the near future. Add to this the prisons that are full of approximately 60,000 Muslim youths, some of them have been there for almost 12 years without being charged.

4.  The international alliance and international pursuit: The regime had no choice but to turn the battle against the mujahid Islamic movement into an international battle, particularly when the United States became convinced that the regime could not survive alone in the face of this fundamentalist campaign.

It was also convinced that this spirit of jihad would most likely turn things upside down in the region and force the United States out of it. This would be followed by the earth-shattering event, which the west trembles at the mere thought of it, which is the establishment of an Islamic caliphate in Egypt.

If God wills it, such a state in Egypt, with all its weight in the heart of the Islamic world, could lead the Islamic world in a jihad against the West. It could also rally the world Muslims around it. Then history would make a new turn, God willing, in the opposite direction against the empire of the United States and the world's Jewish government.

5. The continuation of the battle: Any observer of the progress of the Islamic movement will realize that its battle with the regime continues to this very day. The battle has not stopped in the past 36 years. The fundamentalist movement is either on the attack or in the process of preparing for an attack.

The regime and its media try in vain to convince the people at home and abroad that the battle is over, despite the continuation of the emergency law and the costly security budgets.

All these signs indicate that the regime is still in a state of panic, anticipation, and extreme caution because of the continuing battle and that the situation could explode at any minute. The regime is certain that the international movement produces new generations that the security agencies will not be able to eliminate.

So far Husni Mubarak's government has replaced six Interior Ministers. Each one of them claimed that he would eliminate terrorism, only to find himself ousted and replaced by another person who repeats the same statements.

6. A clear thought and ideology: The Islamic movement has largely succeeded in clarifying the main elements of its ideology, relying on strong evidence from the Koran, the prophet's tradition, and the respected scholars. This provided it with a solid base on which it hoisted its banner, which everyday attracts new advocates, God willing.

7. Weakness of planning and preparations for the jihad actions: We must admit that good planning and preparations have been missing in many of the acts of violence, beginning with the Technical Military College's incident and up to the events in Asyut. Shortcomings in planning were evident.

   If the planning in the killing of Anwar al-Mujahideen, the escape of Isam al-Qamari, the assassination of Rif'at al-Mahjub, and the bombing of the Egyptian Embassy in Islamabad proved to be good, the fundamentalist movement must rid itself of the haphazardness and rashness that continue to dominate many of its actions.

8. The weakness of the message to the people: The fundamentalist movement's message continues to be mostly geared toward the

elite and the specialists. The public and the masses do not understand this message. This is a gap that the jihad movement must strive to fill earnestly, as we will explain later.

If we add to the foregoing the media siege imposed on the message of the jihad movement as well as the campaign of deception mounted by the government media we should realize the extent of the gap in understanding between the jihad movement and the common people.

9.  Failure of some leaders to continue the confrontation: The best proof of this is the initiative made by the Islamic Group leaders in the Turah Prison to suspend military action. We will talk about this in detains, God willing.

10. Conclusion: Has the jihad movement failed or succeeded in the past 36 years? The answer is:

A.  We must admit that the fundamentalist movement's goal of establishing an Islamic government in Egypt is yet to be achieved.

B. The jihad Islamic movement, however, has not set a specific date for achieving this goal. More importantly, this is a goal that could take several generations to achieve. The Crusaders in Palestine and Syria left after two centuries of continued jihad. The Islamic nation at the time had jihad rulers and regular and disciplined armies. It was led by prominent scholars, such as Al-Izz Bin-Abd-al-Salam, Al, Nawawi, and Ibn-Taymiyah, God have mercy on their souls. Despite this, the Crusaders did not leave in 30 or 50 years.

The British occupied Egypt for 70 years. The French occupied Algeria for 120 years.

C. What I see clearly is that the jihad Islamic movement has gone a long way on the road to victory.

1. It possesses a clear-cut ideology based on firm Shari'ah foundations and tangible and realistic facts.

2. It has succeeded in outlining to the youths issues that were absent from the minds of the Muslim masses, such as the supremacy of the Shari'ah, the apostasy of the rulers who do not rule according to God's words, and the necessity of

going against rulers who are affiliated with the enemies of Islam.

3. The jihad movement has exposed the close links between the international regime and the Egyptian regime.

4. The jihad movement has not confined itself to a theoretical debate of these issues. It has put them to practice with an offensive that has shaken the pillars of the regime several times. It also succeeded in assassinating the former President.

5. Based on the above, the jihad movement has strongly influenced the Muslim youth in theory and practice. This has led to the spread of the fundamentalist spirit among large segments of the Egyptian youths. In addition, the fundamentalist movement has influenced broad sectors of the Egyptian people. For instance, one of the defendants in the Al-Mujahideen assassination case told me that one of the lawyers had approached the defendants on trial and asked them enthusiastically and in astonishment: Who are you and where did you come from? By killing Al-Mujahideen, the

Egyptian people have revived hope in the hearts of the nation. Any observer of the jihad Islamic movement could see the clear difference in the strength, clarity of ideology, and activity at the time it started and at the present time.

8. Thus, we could affirm that the jihad movement is growing and making progress in general. It may retreat or relax for a while, but this happens because of the campaigns of brutality or during the periods of siege.

Therefore, the jihad Islamic movement must not stop the resistance and must get the entire nation to participate with it in its battle.

When the second Gulf war occurred, the US military arsenal with its fleets and strike forces moved to the region to oversee the management of its interests by itself. Hence, it transformed its role of hidden mover of events into the role of the Muslims' direct opponent.

The United States denigrated the Islamic shari'ah and insulted the Muslims when the Princedom of Afghanistan, in the words of the mujahid Mullah Muhammad Omar, called on it to present evidence to an Islamic shari'ah court of Bin Ladin's involvement in the terrorist acts.

The US refusal to negotiate with Mullah Omar constituted a "clear insult.

The United States knows in advance what the consequence of its invasion of Afghanistan will be, judging by the lessons of history.

If I die in the battle to defend Islam, my son will rise to avenge me.

The US interest in invading Afghanistan is because of the huge quantities of petroleum under the Caspian Sea, and the US fears that a "fundamentalist belt" would be formed and that Pakistan, which is brimming with Islamist jihadist streams, might be at one end of this belt.

The United States elected to begin by crushing the Chechens by providing the Russian Army with Western aid so that when this campaign ended, it would turn its eyes south to Afghanistan.

The Caucasus and Afghanistan will remain the only Islamist hotbeds against the United States.

Permitting the fundamentalist movement any degree of freedom will shake the foundations of government in many countries.

We have decided that in order to examine the condition of the jihadist movement in Egypt, it is necessary at first to cast a broader look at the heart of the Islamic world. Hence we will divide the discussion in this section of the book into two parts: The First Part is about the enemies of Islam. The second part discusses the Islamist streams.

Several indications are prominent in the US policy towards Islam, notably its basic role in establishing and aiding Israel. Except for Israel, which is in fact a huge US military base, the United States did not resort in the past to conspicuous and intensive military presence to run its affairs in the Middle East until the second Gulf war erupted.

When that happened, the United States rushed to the region with its fleets, its land troops, and air power to manage its own affairs with its own hands under the shadow of its own guns.

With this conspicuous US military presence, several new facts emerged including, first of all, the transformation of the United States from a mover of events from behind a veil to a direct opponent in its battle against the Muslims. Formerly, in both the Arab-Israeli conflict and in managing the internal affairs of other countries, the US administration used to portray itself as an impartial party, or at least as an indirect opponent that merely--as the US alleges-furthers the values of democracy, liberty, and Western interests. Now, however, the role of US power has become clear in attacking Iraq, defending the oil sources, and managing security affairs in some Arab countries.

There is a US intelligence bureau inside the headquarters of the Egyptian State Security Investigation Department that receives daily reports on the number of detainees and those detainees that are released.

There are US military bases at an airport to the west of Cairo, in Wadi Qina, and in the Ra's Binas Naval base.

### The Goals of the US Joint Military Exercises

If you add to the foregoing the joint military exercises such as the Bright Star maneuvers in which the United States and its allies train in ways of invading Egypt's western coast to reach Cairo and attack any fundamentalist regime that assumes power there, then you would understand how prominent this direct role is. In the latest maneuvers, called "Bright Star 99", nine countries participated in addition to the United States, Egypt, and observers from 33 countries.

A total of 73,000 soldiers, 210 combat aircraft, 55 warships, and the aircraft carrier Kennedy, with its full naval and aircraft complement, took part in those exercises. This exercise was described as the largest military maneuver in the world and, according to the commander of the French forces General Harve, "the most important multinational maneuver in the world."

The aim of the maneuvers, as we noted earlier, was a practice run in landing invading forces on Egypt's western coast and then marching southeast towards Cairo, namely, the same route followed by Napoleon Bonaparte during his Egyptian campaign.

The Egyptian forces are not training at this time to repel a likely attack by the Israeli enemy on the Egyptian border as much as they are training to liberate their capital from a likely seizure by a fundamentalist regime. This behavior is an exact repetition of Khedive Tawfiq's behavior towards the British when they invaded Egypt. In other words, the enemy of the Egyptian regime is no longer the country's traditional enemy, Israel, on Egypt's eastern border but the fundamentalists in Cairo.

The Americans limited themselves to this level of conspicuous presence and left the remainder of the task of defending their interests to the Egyptian Government. However, if the Americans feel that they need to undertake direct responsibility for those tasks versus the fundamentalists, then they will not hesitate to do so, as we saw during this latter stage of the Afghan conflict.

The Americans' departure from the role of covert mover of events to assume a direct role in defending their interests has two reasons. The first is the inability-in the US view--of the agents to defend US interests or even to put down the fundamentalist resistance. The second reason is the escalation of events in the region to a degree that has made the United States exercise pressure by itself, using its own troops, weapons, and security agencies.

### The Growth of the Fundamentalist Movement

The fundamentalist movement has grown to such a degree and the resistance to the Zionist presence and to the policies of capitulation to the Zionist enemy has become so strong that the United States has not only decided that its agents are unable to confront their opponent but that this opponent has become so strong that it is necessary to confront this opponent with direct US military power that is present on the battlefront.

This conspicuous US military presence represents an additional step along the path of the policy of (repression by force) that the United States has chosen to pursue in this region. As we noted earlier, the United States has realized that it is impossible to persuade the Muslim nation to accept Israel's existence and its expansionist efforts to establish a Greater Israel and that it is also impossible to continue to rob the Muslims' resources and persuade the Muslims to abandon their demand for a government in accordance with Islamic shari'ah.

The United States, and the global Jewish government that is behind it, have realized that (government by) Islam is the popular demand of the nations of this region, which is considered the heart of the Islamic world. They have realized that it is impossible to compromise on these issues. Hence the United States has decided to dictate its wishes by force, repression, forgery, and misinformation. Finally it has added direct military intervention to all the foregoing methods.

This policy, no matter how long it persists, is a short-term policy that will necessarily provoke repeated eruptions. However, what other alternative do the United States and Israel have?

Allowing the fundamentalist movement any degree of freedom will shake the pillars of the pro-US regimes.

Hence, a decision has been made to resort to the (repression by force) policy in order to close off the volcanic crater in the hope that the imposition of a fait accompli will cause a psychological change among the region's populations and that new generations will grow up who will forget their religious creed, which has been excluded from power, and their rights, which have been usurped.

Furthermore the policy of dictating a fait accompli by force seeks to create new conditions in Muslim lands that it will be very difficult for any Islamist movement seeking to assume power to change except by a monumental effort, particularly in the early days of such a movement's rule.

Nevertheless, history gives the lie to all such plans, for the Crusaders stayed in Greater Syria for 200 years but then had to leave even though they were a model of a settler occupation just like Israel today.

Likewise communism was consigned to history and pursued by curses after 70 years of oppression, obliteration of identity, and population transfers.

It is when one thinks of these points that the importance of continuing the resistance emerges, together with refusing to back down in the face of the US-Zionist schemes to prevent it from achieving its aims and to keep the cause of Islam alive in the hearts of the nation's sons.

The persistence of the resistance will keep the volcano in a state of continual eruption and ready to blow up at the least provocation. The persistence of the resistance will transfer the popular wrath from one generation to another and keep the desire for revenge alive in the people's souls. In contrast, the spread of the concepts of conciliation, acquiescence, and acceptance of the facts will make our generation leave a legacy of despair and a willingness to surrender to the next generation.

## The Global Pursuit of Fundamentalists

If I fall as a martyr in the defense of Islam, my son Muhammad will avenge me, but if I am finished politically and I spend my time arguing with governments about some partial solutions, what will motivate my son to take up my weapons after I have sold these weapons in the bargains' market? More important than all the foregoing is the fact that resistance is a duty imposed by shari'ah.

In the wake of the USSR's collapse, the United States monopolized its military superiority to dictate its wishes to numerous governments and, as a result, has succeeded in imposing security agreements on many countries.

In this way the power of the governments that are affiliated with the United States grew in the sphere of pursuing the mujahideen in many countries. Doubtlessly this had an impact on the fundamentalist movement. Still this has been a new challenge that the jihadist movement confronted with methods that can reduce its impact. It did this by turning the United States into a target.

We should not fail to mention at this point the Sharm al-Shaykh conference that was held in March 1996 and was attended by the Arab countries--except for Sudan, Iraq, Syria, and Lebanon-the United States, Russia, and many Western countries to agree on ensuring that no Islamist attacks could be carried out against Israel.

It was a very insulting and humiliating spectacle and reminds me of this verse by Al-Mutanabbi:

> *He who holds his own worth too light, Will find further humiliation easy to bear, For you cannot make a person feel pain From a new wound if he is already dead.*

That conference adopted both public resolutions and secret security cooperation agreements to ensure Israeli security.

Under US tutelage and guidance the Arab interior ministers held conferences that finally produced an agreement to combat terrorism. And each year they have been adding a new restrictive clause to this agreement.

The United States was not satisfied merely with agreements and conferences but prodded its own organization (the United Nations) to adopt a resolution imposing economic sanctions on Afghanistan because it refused to hand over the persons wanted by the United States, notably Usama Bin Ladin.

## Mullah Omar's Defiance of the United States

In the 1990s the United States confronted a new phenomenon that represented a fierce challenge to its dominance and arrogance, namely, the emergence of two Islamic states that liberated their territory under the slogan of jihad in the cause of God against the infidel occupiers of Muslim lands.

Those two countries were Afghanistan and Chechnya. The matter did not stop there, for these two emerging countries became the safe haven and destination of emigrants and mujahideen from various parts of the world or what the United States describes as Arab Afghans, fundamentalists, terrorists, and so on.

The defiance shown by the Islamic principality of Afghanistan, under the leadership of "Prince of the Faithful, the mujahid Mullah Mohammad Omar", when it refused to comply with the US request to hand over Usama Bin Ladin and his companions, and its firm steadfastness in continuing to reject this request even in the wake of the US missile strikes against Afghan territory, represented a challenge that the United States could neither absorb nor adapt to.

At the same time the Chechen mujahideen's defiance of Russia, their insistence on liberating the Muslim Caucasus, and their determination to complete the jihad begun by Imam Shamil (Basayev), may he rest in peace, against Czarist Russia posed a great threat to the influence and interests of the United States, for the Caucasus floats on a sea of petroleum whose estimated reserves are no less than the oil reserves in the Arabian Gulf, especially as the US influence in Central Asia is increasing and taking the form of military bases, spy stations, oil companies, and joint maneuvers.

**The Reasons for the War on Afghanistan**

The liberation of the Caucasus would constitute a hotbed of jihad (or fundamentalism as the United States describes it) and that region would become the shelter of thousands of Muslim mujahideen from various parts of the Islamic world, particularly Arab parts. This poses a direct threat to the United States represented by the growing support for the jihadist movement everywhere in the Islamic world.

If the Chechens and other Caucasian mujahideen reach the shores of the oil-rich Caspian Sea, the only thing that will separate them from Afghanistan will be the neutral state of Turkmenistan.

This will form a mujahid Islamic belt to the south of Russia that will be connected in the east to Pakistan, which is brimming with mujahideen movements in Kashmir. The belt will be linked to the south with Iran and Turkey that are sympathetic to the Muslims of Central Asia. This will break the cordon that is struck around the Muslim Caucasus and allow it to communicate with the Islamic world in general,

Furthermore the liberation of the Muslim Caucasus will lead to the fragmentation of the Russian Federation and will help escalate the jihad movements that already exist in the republics of Uzbekistan and Tajikistan, whose governments get Russian backing against those jihadist movements.

The fragmentation of the Russian Federation on the rock of the fundamentalist movement and at the hands of the Muslims of the Caucasus and Central Asia will topple a basic ally of the United States in its battle against the Islamic jihadist reawakening.

For this reason the United States chose to begin by crushing the Chechens by providing Western financing for the Russian Army so that when this brutal campaign against the Chechen mujahideen is completed, the campaign can move southwards to Afghanistan either by the action of former Soviet republics that are US agents or with the participation of US troops under the guise of combating terrorism, drug trafficking, and the claims about liberating that region's women.

In this way the United States will have destroyed the two last remaining hotbeds of resistance to it in the Islamic world. For this reason the United States remained silent about the brutal massacres that were carried out in Chechnya and the volcanic fire that was poured on the head of this small republic.

Those massacres were unlike anything seen since World War II. Apart from some expressions of denunciation and protest designed to avert criticism against itself, the United States maintained that the Chechen issue was a domestic Russian problem. One should note the fact that there was Jewish-Russian cooperation in the anti-Chechnya campaign. This was proven when Jewish security experts fell into the hands of the Chechen mujahideen.

This means that the same America that fights against us in Egypt and backs Israel in the heart of the Islamic world is also leading the battle against us in Chechnya, the Caucasus, and also in Somalia where 13,000 Somali nationals were killed in the course of what the United States alleged was its campaign to distribute foodstuffs in Somalia.

In the name of food aid, the United States perpetrated hideous acts against the Somalis, acts that came to light only later. Detainees were tortured and their honor violated at the hands of the international coalition forces that allegedly came to rescue Somalia.

In Afghanistan the United States publicly sflouted the Islamic shari'ah when Afghanistan called on it to submit evidence against Shaykh Usama Bin Ladin to a shari'ah court. The US response was that Washington does not recognize shari'ah courts and demands that Usama Bin Ladin be handed over to a country where he can face justice.

Such is the United States, and such is its policy.

### Jihadist Movements

This section is two parts:

The first part speaks about the general characteristics of jihadist movements and the second is about the initiative to halt military operations.

Brother Abu-Salman al-Maghribi wrote in memory of one of the bombers of the US Embassy in Nairobi in August 1998.

> *Your good action caused flags to fly at half-mast,*
> *And your chaste face smashed idols.*
> *You said goodbye to lions and their young cubs*
> *And strode through a door where you were an imam.*
> *Finding other courses of endeavor crowded,*
> *You selected a course where there was no crowd*
> *With high resolve, you looked with disdain on death*
> *And defeated the massive army of infidelity and doubt.*

The fundamentalist movement has made its goal clear, namely, to topple the government and establish an Islamic state.

The fundamentalist movement realizes that a clash between it and the Jewish-US alliance is inevitable and understands that this is its destiny and duty; that this is its battle that it has been waging and will wage further still.

## The Initiative To Halt Military Action

The (prophet's companion) Abdallah Bin-al-Zubayr went into his mother's house and complained to her that the people were letting him down and joining Al-Hajjaj (Bin-al-Zubayr's enemy, early Muslim commander and province governor under the Omayyad Caliphate). Even his sons and other relatives had joined Al-Hajjaj and he had only a few men left with him who could not endure long in battle. He told her that the opponents were willing to give him any worldly goods he wanted if he abandoned the fight and he asked for her opinion.

His mother replied: Son, you know yourself better. If you are convinced that you are right and that you are advocating a rightful course of action, then endure. Your companions were killed defending what is right.

Do not let the Omayyad young men manipulate your destiny. If you sense in yourself a desire for worldly goods, then you are an unworthy Muslim and your soul will perish and you will cause the souls of those who die along with you to perish. If you are right, then it is not religion that is weak. Do you think that you can live forever? Death is better.

Abdallah Bin-al-Zubayr approached his mother and kissed the top of her head and said: By God, this is also my opinion." (from the counsel that Asma Bint-Abu-Bakr, may they both reside in God's pleasure, gave to her son on the eve of his death in battle)

Sayyid Qutb, the most prominent theoretician of the fundamentalist movements, said: "Brother, push ahead, for your path is soaked in blood. Do not turn your head right or left but look only up to heaven."

The objective has been somewhat shaken by the fact that the Islamic Group was dragged into a stance where it halted armed jihadist action under the name of (the initiative to halt military operations). This initiative has had serious repercussions. Because all persons, those who are and those who are not connected with the issue, have begun debating the initiative, I have decided to discuss it with some frankness and in some detail. I apologize to my brothers in the Islamic Group-whom I respect and love-for disagreeing with their view and criticizing their opinions. However, in my efforts to properly interpret shari'ah, I find that doing what is right is dearer to me than these brothers' love.

The beginnings of the no-violence initiative, or the halting of operations, began with an appeal made by Khalid Ibrahim, leader of the Islamic Group's Aswan branch, who was a defendant in the Islamic Group case in Aswan in April 1996. He notes that the Islamic Group made another appeal in July 1997 in the name of the Islamic Group's leaders who are still serving jail terms at the Turrah and al-Aqrab prisons. It called on the Islamic Group's members inside Egypt and abroad to halt military operations and to stop issuing statements inciting such operations. The Islamic Group asked the government to respond to its initiative.

In the words of then Interior Minister Hasan al-Alfi, the government said that it does not pay attention to such initiatives that merely seek to reduce the jail terms of the group's members and, additionally, the government does not deal with outlaws.

Al-Alfi's successor Habib al-Adli announced that the government does not negotiate with anyone but can release anyone who repents and undertakes to abandon violence and terrorism.

## Questions About the Initiative To Halt Violent Operations

After the introduction that we mentioned above, we believe that we should present the initiative issue in the form of answers to the following questions:

a.      What do the Islamic Group's members have to say about the initiative?

b.      -What description can be given to the initiative?

c.      How convincing are the justifications to make such an initiative?

d.      What effects has the initiative had so far?

What do the Islamic Group's members have to say about the initiative?

The reader might be surprised that I should begin with this formalistic question but I elected to do so because the answer can reveal facts that are useful in researching this initiative.

1. The first Islamic Group spokesman to make this initiative was Khalid Ibrahim, the Islamic

Group's leader in Aswan. He made the initiative during his trial in April 1996. The Lawyer Muntasir al-Zayyat encouraged him to make this initiative, promoted it, and published it in the media. Al-Zayyat alleged at that time that he was waiting for responses to the initiative from the brothers abroad.

2. Afterwards Muhammad Abd-al-Alim spoke on behalf of the Islamic Group leaders during his trial in July 1997 in the case of the bombings of banks. The counsel for the defense was again Muntasir al-Zayyat. Muhammad Abd-al-Alim quoted several announcements by the group's leaders. In the first announcement, they called on the group's members in Egypt and abroad to halt military operations and to stop issuing statements that incite such operations.

In a second announcement, they declared that it is not right to commit unjust aggression against the Copts without rightful cause. In a third announcement, they reaffirmed their adherence to halting military operations and any inciting statements both inside Egypt and abroad. They declared that this announcement was not the result of negotiations with the security agencies or other departments but was made for the good of Islam and the Muslims.

When Dr. Omar Abdel Rahman, from his jail in the United States, issued a statement supporting the aforementioned initiative that was made by the jailed Islamic Group leaders, they responded to it and reaffirmed their earlier position in their fifth statement which declared: "The brothers in the Turrah jail express thanks to their shaykh Dr. Omar Abdel Rahman for his enlightened and courageous stance on the initiative to halt the operations. His stance is in harmony with the enlightened positions to which they have always been accustomed to see him adopt for he seeks to avoid bloodshed and when he calls on God for assistance, he does it in an enlightened way, and God has rewarded him. We call on intermediaries to carry out good offices to seek his release from his jail."

The Islamic Group leaders in the Turrah jail sent a cable to the leaders of the country's political parties and other public personalities. It was published in the Al-Wafd newspaper and was given a banner headline. The statement read: "We have sought to halt the fighting to avoid shedding the blood of the population. We hope to get your support for our initiative. We appeal to the President and the government to respond and interact with this initiative."

Later on the brothers at the Turrah jail issued a response to Dr. Omar Abdel Rahman's withdrawal of his support for the initiative. We will talk about this when we present Abdel Rahman's statements.

3. Usamah Rushdi, on the occasion of his acquittal of the Luxor incident that occurred on November 17, 1997, also spoke about the initiative. He discussed it again in his response to brother Rifa'i Taha, the Islamic Group's military commander. This response arrived in Cairo from Damascus four months ago. I read an interview with Usamah Rushdi in Al-Sharq al-Awsat, parts of which I am going to relate because it gives another dimension to the ideological changes that occurred within the ranks of the Islamic Group. Rushdi believes that Shaykh Omar Abdel Rahman changed his mind about the initiative and withdrew his support for it because he did not get enough information about the situation.

Rushdi says: "Regarding the shaykh's change of mind and his withdrawal of support for the initiative that was made by the brothers in Egypt three years ago, the shaykh reached this conclusion because he received information that tens of thousands of detainees were still held in jail and tortured. "

Although Rushdi believes that the insufficient information that the shaykh receives is the reason why he withdrew his support for the initiative, he admits that the situation in Egypt is bad and that the government is still using the same methods.

Rushdi says: "Regarding the initiative to halt armed action, the most optimistic among the Islamic Group's members are frustrated because the regime has dragged its feet in carrying out the actions that this initiative should entail (istihqaqat al-mubadarah). Human rights violations continue to occur in the prisons and the humanitarian needs of the detainees and their families are disregarded."

### A Turnabout in Constants

Rushdi uses the word "istihqaq" (here meaning action that should come as a response to the no-violence initiative) This is a strange term and I do not know what he means by it.

Rushdi also says that "our brothers are subjected to torture and banishment in jail and detention camps and are deprived of any legal or political guarantees."

When the interviewer asks Rushdi if "the release of 7,000 detainees and treating the rest

143

of the prisoners in a more humane way is not considered a positive outcome", Rushdi replies: "This figure is not generally accepted. Furthermore thousands of Islamic Group members are being detained without a charge or trial. Some have already spent more than 10 years in jail."

I do not know why Rushdi regards the information on which Shaykh Omar Abdel Rahman based his withdrawal of support for the initiative as insufficient although he acknowledges that this information is true. Or does he mean some other information? He says that the shaykh withdrew his support for the initiative in line with information he received about the continuing torture of tens of thousands of detainees. Rushdi describes this information as insufficient, but then he comes backs and asserts that thousands of the Islamic Group's members are detained and suffer torture and banishment.

Rushdi believes that the Egyptian Government should find a solution to Omar Abdel Rahman's problem and says: "I maintain that the Egyptian Government is guilty of a major shortcoming by not intervening to safeguard the shaykh, guarantee his humanitarian rights inside his US jail, and find a solution to his case because, in the final count, he is an Egyptian

144

national, a Muslim scholar, and a professor at Al-Azhar university. Finally he is a blind and sick old man. His continued detention and the inhuman way in which he is treated will continue to be a source of tension on all levels."

The interviewer asks Rushdi: "In your view, what can guarantee that Omar Abdel Rahman will not become a nuisance to Egypt itself if it supports him and asks that he be handed over to it?"

Rushdi answers: "We have known the shaykh always to stand by his sons and brothers. In my assessment, the shaykh will not defy the consensus over continuing and acting on the (no-violence) initiative. Hence, his return to Egypt would promote the current calm situation and would defuse a major source of Islamic anger and tension on the international scene."

He then proposes a deal by which Omar Abdel Rahman would be released in exchange for not bothering the Egyptian Government but would promote calm and defuse tensions, not only in Egypt but throughout the world. He would support the Islamic Group's consensus (on the no-violence initiative).

I cannot see where this consensus lies since people of the stature of Omar Abdel Rahman and Rifa'i Taha oppose the initiative?

I remember a scene that occurred 17 years ago during the first week of September 1983. Shaykh Omar Abdel Rahman was roaring in the courtroom and speaking these words to the judge: "I am a Muslim who lives only for his religion and is prepared to die for it. I can never remain silent while Islam is being fought on all fronts."

The fundamentalist Usamah Rushdi then compares the Egyptian state to the father in a family and the Muslim youths as its sons, this being a new relationship that has grown out of the new ideas that have started to emerge. He then implies that the Islamic Group might adhere to Egypt's laws and constitution.

The journalist interviewing him asks: "What guarantees could the Islamic Group provide to demonstrate its adherence to the laws and the constitution?"

Rushdi answers in the manner of a politician who does not wish to shut the door to further discussion: "Our brothers are suffering torture in jail and banishment to remote prison camps. They are deprived of any legal, humanitarian, or political guarantees. You cannot ask them for guarantees while this condition persists. First give me my rights and then ask me to give guarantees."

An Islamic Group spokesman, believed to be Muntasir al-Zayyat, made the following statement to a Libyan magazine that is a mouthpiece of the Libyan Islamic Combat Group:

- The initiative is a legitimate necessity that has an objective that will be fulfilled in the future.

- The initiative does not mean that the Islamic Group has abandoned its tenets, nor does it constitute a contradiction of the concept of jihad.

- It does not signify that the Islamic Group is placating the ruling regimes or approving of these regimes' policies.

- There is no longer any point to continuing the armed operations.

- The Islamic Group was compelled to begin the armed operations in self-defense to halt the policy of killing its leaders and to stop the aggression against itself.

- A new policy is necessary in the hope that the government would end its attacks. If the regime does not respond, the door is still open (to resume operations). The same party that shut the door can reopen it but only after the regime's true nature becomes exposed to everyone.

- The regime's surveillance agencies have ascertained the success of the policy of "drying up the terrorists' (financial) resources. The Islamic Group's stance confirms this fact.

- These policies have proven their efficacy in dealing with the Islamist stream.

- It is expected that the regime will soon sense the urgent need to remove its yoke of oppression from the necks of the population and the Islamists.

- The Islamic Group has the right to make its own decision on halting armed operations.

- The above does not prevent the Islamic Group from changing its stance once again.

- Setting slogans aside, the existing facts do not enable the Islamic Group to continue its confrontation with the regime.

- It was hoped at first that the initiative would bring some results but these hopes have been dashed and do not seem likely to be attained.

- The Islamic Group's main objective is to have a presence in the sphere of the call to the faith and in charitable social work among the Muslim masses.

- Continuing the current confrontation does harm and no benefit can be gained from it.

- If a group refrains from carrying out jihad for a while, this does not mean that it has completely abandoned the concept of this religious duty.

- Some of the group's leaders believe that the initiative is useless but it is the view of the majority that is followed.

Furthermore Dr. Omar Abdel Rahman made a statement after the initiative was made under the slogan "Halt (the operations) for the sake of God's pleasure."

However, early in June 2000 Dr. Omar Abdel Rahman issued a statement from his jail that was relayed by his lawyer Lynn Stewart in which she said that Shaykh Omar was withdrawing his support for the no-violence initiative because it had not brought any positive results for the Islamists. Stewart cited Abdel Rahman as saying: "There has been no progress. Thousands of detainees are still in jail, the military tribunals are still prosecuting people, and the death penalty continues to be carried out."

Dr. Omar Abdel Rahman's clear assessment of the situation is an eloquent reply to the third statement issued by the brother leaders in the Turrah jail in which they said that they "cling to their position on halting armed operations and any announcements that incite armed operations inside Egypt and abroad." They noted that this "announcement is not the product of negotiation with the security services or other government departments but is in line with Islamic shari'ah and serves the interests of the Muslims."

Several days later Muntasir al-Zayyat held a news conference at his office in which he cast doubt on the statement attributed to Shaykh Abdel Rahman by his lawyer. He refused to show the journalists Dr. Omar Abdel Rahman's letter to the Islamic Group's leaders in the Turrah prison.

Al-Zayyat told the journalists that the jailed group leaders sent a message to Shaykh Omar explaining their position on the initiative. The following persons signed the letter: Najih Ibrahim, Ali al-Sharif, Isam Darbalah, Hamdi Abd-al-Rahman, Fu'ad al-Dawalibi, Karam Zuhdi, and Asim Abd-al-Majid. Al-Sharq al-Awsat noticed that Abbud al-Zumar did not sign the letter.

Less than one week later the newspapers published a response from Shaykh Omar Abdel Rahman replying to the statement of the group's leaders.

Al-Sharq al-Awsat reported: "Omar Abdel Rahman, spiritual leader of the Islamic Group, the largest fundamentalist group in Egypt, has reiterated his withdrawal of support for the initiative to halt violence that was declared by the group's traditional leaders who are serving jail terms.

He noted that he did not abolish the initiative but simply withdrew his support for it."

Omar Abdel Rahman said in a signed statement, a copy of which was received by Al-Sharq al-Awsat, that he asked that his statements be published through his US lawyer Lynn Stewart, after some fundamentalists questioned whether the statements attributed to him were really his.

Stewart received the following from Abd-al-Rahman: "I have not abolished the initiative but I have withdrawn my support for it. I have made my view clear but left the issue to my brothers to debate among themselves as to how useful the initiative is."

Omar Abdel Rahman said: "All the statements attributed to me by my lawyer Lynn Stewart are true and have actually come from me."

It is important here to stop and examine the ease and flexibility with which Muntasir al-Zayyat can operate under the aegis of governmental facilities. Visits to prisoners have been banned for four years, dozens are quietly killed inside their jails, and preachers are prohibited in accordance with Article 201 of the Penalty Code from protesting against administrative laws and decisions.

The country continues to languish under the burden of the Emergency Law, Muslim young men are abducted in various countries and brought back to Egypt, the government then conceals them for long months before revealing their presence in the country, as in the case of Ahmad Salamah and Isam Muhammad Hafiz. Sometimes the government denies that it knows anything about their fate as in the case of Tal'at Fu'ad and brother Muhammad al-Zawahiri.

While all this is happening, Muntasir al-Zayyat hastens to the Turrah prison, meets with the Islamic Group's leaders, delivers to them a letter from Umar Abd-al-Rahman, gets a statement from them in response to the letter and also gets a letter from them to carry to Shaykh Umar. He returns from jail on the same day, contacts the newspapers, and tells them about the statement issued by the jailed brothers and their letter to Dr. Umar. He then holds a news conference at his office (just imagine this) and makes his views known on Shaykh Umar's statements and Rifa'i Taha's statements on the initiative (we will have more to say about this later). He refuses to let the journalists know the contents of Shaykh Umar's letter although US and Egyptian security agencies are informed of the contents. The Egyptian people, however, are not supposed to know the truth of Shaykh Umar's letter to his brothers.

Does this not make you want to pause, think, and ask why?

While Muntasir al-Zayyat enjoys these amazing privileges in Egypt, New York City's Assistant District Attorney Patrick Fitzgerald sent a letter to the lawyer Lynn Stewart and the rest of the shaykh's defense team banning them from visiting the shaykh or talking with him on the telephone. This happened after Lynn Stewart held a news conference-on the shaykh's request-in which she announced that the shaykh had withdrawn his support for the initiative to halt armed operations. Just imagine this harmonious Egyptian-US coordination vis-a-vis the initiative.

Brother Rifa'i Ahmad Taha also commented on the initiative. He rejected it when it was first made and later repeated his rejection after Shaykh Umar announced that he was withdrawing his support for it. He told Al-Sharq al-Awsat: "Regarding the case of Umar Abd-al-Rahman, the Islamic Group's spiritual leader who is detained in a US jail, the policy of talking and making threats is over. We will address the United States in a language that it understands. We will break his shackles and release him from captivity. I believe that the time to do so is drawing near."

Asked if the Islamic Group might revise its past errors, Rifa'i Taha said: "In answer to your question-if I have understood it correctly--if the Islamic Group has altered its methods and is revising its past errors, my answer is this: The Islamic Group does not believe that it made errors in the past whether in its call to jihad, in its promotion of virtue and prohibition of vice, or in its call to God's religion."

Muntasir al-Zayyat hastened to hold a news conference in which he responded to Rifa'i Ahmad Taha's remarks. Al-Zayyat said: "The Islamic Group's leaders have the highest respect for Taha and appreciate his role in shouldering the group's tasks and responsibilities at one time.

However, at this time he represents only his own personal view that is not binding on the Islamic Group as a whole."

Al-Zayyat noted that decision-making within the group is the domain of its traditional leaders, namely, those who are in jail in Egypt and the group's shura (consultative) council abroad that is chaired by Mustafa Hamzah."

Karam Zuhdi also spoke about the initiative to halt armed operations. In a news conference Muntasir al-Zayyat cited Zuhdi as saying: "If fighting and armed operations have not helped the Islamic Group to achieve its aims over all those years, then it must seek other methods of operation."

If the above statement really came from Karam Zuhdi, this means that the Islamic Group has abandoned fighting as a method of operation and has, indeed, also abandoned its advocacy of such armed operations both inside and outside Egypt. In exchange for what has it done so? What is the alternative? Does the alternative consist of repeated requests to the government, made by the people who presented the initiative, to show responsiveness to their initiative? Does the alternative consist of asking the leaders of the political parties to intercede with the government to make it respond to their initiative?

Is this the Islamic Group's alternative method to jihad and incitement to jihad? Does the work of the jihadist groups-that is governed by shari'ah, an understanding of the jurisprudence of the historical imams, the nation's ulema, and proof of adherence to shari'ah-consist nowadays of repeatedly soliciting the secular governments to give us permission to establish an Islamic state?

### Observations on Al-Zayyat

Muntasir al-Zayyat has also spoken in the name of the Islamic Group. When we speak about this man, we need to make several observations.

a) Muntasir al-Zayyat has for a long time promoted the idea of halting jihad action against the government and its US and Jewish allies inside and outside Egypt. Since Abd-al-Halim Musa's term as Interior Minister, Al-Zayyat has taken part in numerous communications on this issue.

b) Any observer can notice that Muntasir al-Zayyat enjoys privileges unavailable even to many Egyptian ministers. He can, on the same day that he makes the request, enter any of Egypt's long-established jails and pass through all security checks. He then holds meetings inside these jails with the most dangerous anti-government figures, delivers messages to them from abroad, and takes out messages and statements from them. He then holds news conferences to publish and distribute these messages and statements to the media. He declares that he is the agent of the Islamic

Group's traditional leaders and the person authorized to speak on their behalf. He conducts interviews on the radio and the satellite channels in this capacity.

Indeed Al-Zayyat is almost the only channel of communication between the jailed Islamic Group's leaders and the outside world. Whatever messages they receive pass through him and whatever statements they issue, he carries in his pocket or we listen to them through his words.

If you add to this the fact that officials of the State Security Investigation Department told Al-Zayyat before he was released from jail at the end of his detention in connection with the Lawyers Association's strike that if he crossed certain red lines, he would cost them only a few pennies, that is, the price of one bullet, you would then grasp a new dimension of the group's initiative to halt armed operations.

In his movements Muntasir al-Zayyat enjoys the backing and authorization of the jailed Islamic Group's leaders. This backing and authorization has been repeated on several occasions.

On 5 January 1998 Al-Zayyat declared that he was retiring completely from public political life and that he would no longer represent defendants in cases connected with the religious groups, citing as a reason the alleged fact that the leaders abroad let him down and did not respond to his good offices to halt the violence.

He issued a statement in which he said: "The violence still rages in my country and the political climate is still complicated. I have tried along with others to promote a halt to violence and to end the bloodshed. I have never been a hired lawyer who defends for the sake of payment but rather I have done this as a vocation, a calling. I have had discussions with many people, notably the Islamic Group leaders who are serving jail sentences at the Turrah prison in connection with the Al-Mujahideen case. We have tried to express legitimate Islamic aspirations but these aspirations were lost amid the smoke of shells and the noise of bullets."

He added: "The cause to which I have devoted myself is no longer clear. Although I have tolerated a great burden and walked through thorns and mine fields for 20 years during which I was caught between the government's hammer and the anvil of the religious groups, yet I have always sought to be clear in my work, speech, and transactions without running afoul of the law by having illegal relationships since I was released from jail in connection with the Al-Jihad case in 1984."

Muntasir continued: "I have suffered a lot from the intransigence of the brothers abroad and their inability to adopt daring resolutions or develop new methods of action. Every idea has its own tone of address, method, and strategy. As Islamists we used to reap much benefit when we exercised public call to the faith at mosques and Islamic forums. Despite all the obstacles, violence cannot be the remedy. If violence is sometimes justified, it has no justification if it is no longer rooted in logic and sound argument and turns into an indiscriminate act conducted against innocent people just as happened in Luxor."

### Muslim Brotherhood and Other Jihadist Movements

The Muslim Brotherhood is growing organizationally but is committing suicide ideologically and politically. The history of the Muslim Brotherhood is full of mistakes and failures and adds that the mistakes committed by the biggest Islamic movement in the world prompted me to write "The Muslim Brotherhood's Bitter Harvest in 60 Years. " (Al-

Hisad al-Murr lil Al-Ikhwan al-Muslimin fi Sittin Aman.)

I was sharply criticized by his brothers in the fundamentalist movements because of the book "The Bitter Harvest" because I concentrated on the bad deeds of the Muslim Brotherhood without mentioning any of their good deeds. Some fundamentalists claim that I insulted Muslim Brotherhood founder and general guide Shaykh Hasan al-Banna (may God have mercy on him. Bitter Harvest is as a human judgement that does not claim be infallible. Oh Muslim Brotherhood youth, it is up to you to carry out a corrective renaissance within

O ye who believe! Fear God and be with those who are true (in word and deed).

It was not fitting for the people of Medina and the Bedouin Arabs of the neighborhood to refuse to follow God's Apostle, nor to prefer their own lives to his: because not nothing could they suffer or do, but was reckoned to their credit as a deed of righteousness, -- Whether they suffered thirst, or fatigue, or hunger, in the Cause of God, or trod paths to raise the ire of the unbelievers, or received any injury, whatever from any enemy: For God suffereth not the reward to be lost of those who do good;--

Nor they could they spend anything (For the Cause)--small or great--Nor cut across a valley, but the deed is inscribed to their credit; that God may requite their deed with the best possible reward).

Without a doubt, the Muslim Brotherhood is the biggest Islamic movement in the modern age. It is also the first that was established in the Arab world. The Muslim Brotherhood has been able to spread worldwide and to survive despite the obstacles and difficulties it has faced sometimes.

But the situation in which the Muslim Brotherhood has brought itself in the Muslim world in general and in Egypt in particular requires study and contemplation. Maybe the Muslim Brotherhood is growing organizationally but it is committing suicide ideologically and politically.

One of the main reasons for this political and ideological suicide was the Muslim Brotherhood's pledge of allegiance to the President of the Republic (Husni Mubarak) in 1987.

The MB has reneged on its history of struggle and what this history contains in terms of the blood of the martyrs, the wounds of the detainees, and the agony of the fugitives. Not only that, the MB has also reneged on its principles and creed. The MB is drifting away from its history, creating a new generation who only cares about worldly things now and in the future.

This pledge of alliance was one of the important reasons that I wrote "The Muslim Brotherhood's Bitter Harvest in Sixty Years." Criticism has been leveled at me because of this book.

Some of my brothers have blamed me because of the book's contents. Some of them are proud of their relationship both with me and with the Muslim Brotherhood. Their criticism was that this book is unfair because it pinpoints the mistakes of the Muslim Brotherhood and does not mention any of their good deeds although their history is full of good deeds.

They even accused me of denying some of the Muslim Brotherhood's great deeds and that I have insulted Shaykh Hasan al-Banna (may God have mercy on him)--something that is not proper by someone who belongs to the

Islamic movement and who knows the importance and virtues of Shaykh Al-Banna.

My response to them is as follows:

1. This book is a human judgment that does not claim to be infallible and that might make mistakes and contain all human shortcomings.

2. With your admission you agree with me that the Muslim Brotherhood have made mistakes that are tantamount to crimes that must be punished. They have also carried out many good acts that elevate them to the status of saints. I have waited for the Muslim Brotherhood to correct their mistakes or to draw the attention of the young generation to these mistakes. I have only found from you criticism in your private councils and silence and negativity in enlightening the young generation.

3. My book is not a comprehensive review of the Muslim Brotherhood so that it will be criticized for ignoring their good deeds. That is why I did not call the book 'The Muslim Brotherhood in the Balance.' My book is a warning, especially to the Muslim youth, not to slide into the same slope until they reach the bottom to which the Muslim Brotherhood have slid, while these youth think they are

supporting Islam and struggling for the sake of God."

I have given the Muslim Brotherhood an example. I said I am like a doctor who is treating a patient suffering from stomach cancer that might kill him. It is not acceptable for the doctor to tell the patient that his brain is good, his heart is good, his kidneys are good, all his organs are good except the stomach, which has cancer. It is the duty of the doctor to warn the patient that he might die from a dangerous disease, that he must treat himself or else he will die, and that his good heart, brain, and organs will not help him if the cancer is not excised from his stomach.

4. I do not deny that the book contains some phrases in the book that need to be deleted or amended, such as "the Jews have been in Palestine since 1948 but the Muslim Brotherhood have never disturbed them for 44 years because the government has not allowed them to do this.

I testify that the Muslim Brotherhood have fought the Jews and that their youth are still fighting them in Palestine until now.

I do not deny that there are some unnecessary phrases in the book; however, their removal will not affect the topic of the book. I have revised the book twice and have thought of publishing a second edition. I do not know whether God will help me to do this or not.

Concerning my criticism of Shaykh Hasan al-Banna (may God have mercy on him), I was prompted by two things:

First, Shaykh Hasan al-Banna (may God have mercy on him) was an historic public figure who must be studied by anyone critical of the Muslim Brotherhood. I did not sanctify Shaykh Hasan al-Banna, as many Muslim Brothers have done.

I did not consider him deceptive and fallacious, as secularists and communists have done. I just studied and criticized his work according to my best ability, reporting on him and the Muslim Brotherhood as best as I could. Regrettably, no Muslim Brotherhood leader has answered me, as far as I know.

Second, many of those who came after Hasan al-Banna (may God have mercy on him) were justifying their mistakes by saying Hasan al-Banna did this and that before them. Therefore, it was necessary to study the use of (the words and deeds of) Hasan al-Banna as a precedent. The course of the people of the Sunna (Sunni

Muslims) is to know righteousness in order to know its men and not to know men in order to know righteousness.

5. However, after the publication of this book, the Muslim Brotherhood have regrettably committed several doctrinal mistakes. They issued statements, including a statement entitled 'Statement from the Muslim Brotherhood to the People.' They started speaking about a new fiqh (new jurisprudence) alien to the scholars of Islam and in which they equated Muslims and with non-Muslims in all the material, moral, civilian, and political rights of citizenship. Our brother Ahmad Abd-al-Salam Shahin responded to them in his book 'Fath al-Rahman fi al-Rad ala Bayan al-Ikhwan'.

In a previous statement, the Muslim Brotherhood said they believe the Christians have the right to hold all the state's posts except the post of the President of the Republic. Why? In other words, the Muslim Brotherhood don't mind if the Egyptian Prime Minister is a Christian! Why not also a Jew? We do have Jews in Egypt. Or the issue is a political propaganda and not principles, as they claim?

6. On the level of the major events facing the Muslim nation, the Muslim Brotherhood in general and those in Egypt in particular have chosen to be passive and to abandon jihad for the sake of God, although jihad is the greatest duty of Islam. This is despite all the catastrophes that have befallen our nation and despite the US and Jewish occupation of our lands and the tyranny of the (local) rulers and their aggression on Muslims.

7. Therefore, the Muslim Brotherhood youth must carry out a corrective renaissance within their societies. They must affirm the need to return to the pure doctrine of the righteous predecessors, to adhere to the unchanging rules of the shari'ah, to stop inventing what they call the "new fiqh," and to stand in one line with their brother mujahideen everywhere.

8. The Muslim Brotherhood youth must realize that the new crusader onslaught will not be pleased with them until they join the faith of the infidels and that all the tricks of politics and pacification will not work. It is better for the youth of Islam to carry arms and defend their religion with pride and dignity instead of living in humiliation in the empire of the New World order.

9. The forces of jihad are gathering these days and are forming a new reality that has waged battles against the Western infidels and their local agents.

Acquittal of 194 out of 302 defendants in the Al-Mujahideen (assassination) case was more of a surprise to the security Services than to the Islamists

The Muslim Brotherhood misled the ruling regime by assuring Al-Mujahideen that the fundamentalist movements did not pose any threat to his regime. Events in the Egyptian street have proved that the fundamentalist movements will continue to be capable of introducing change. The assassination of Al-Mujahideen was a strong blow to the US plan for the region.

The military trial is an example of the repeated confrontations between the Islamists and so-called military secularism, but the verdicts of the president of court, counselor Abd-al-Ghaffar, were fair.

After the investigation period was over and the prosecutor completed his investigations, the defendants were referred to court in the biggest case in the history of the Egyptian judiciary.

The prosecutor sent 302 defendants to court. The proceedings of the trial started approximately two years after the assassination of Al-Mujahideen.

The trial was unique and full of surprises. But the most important events in the trial were 1) the delivery by Dr. Omar Abdel Rahman of his famous testimony for three days, and 2) the historic testimony by Shaykh Salah Abu-Isma'il (may God have mercy on him).

Shaykh Omar Abdel Rahman later on published his testimony in a book entitled "A word of Truth."

Dr. Omar Abdel Rahman reviewed the issues of shari'ah and jihad (holy war) in detail, citing the Koran and the Sunnah (sayings and doings of Prophet Muhammad) and the consensus of the nation's religious scholars. He responded to the prosecutor's indictment and the Al-Azhar report that the prosecutor has used. This testimony jeopardized Dr. Omar Abdel Rahman's legal position because it contained evidence of his support for ' jihad and establishing the shari'ah. The judge warned him that his words were very dangerous because the words of his lawyers could be retracted but his words could not.

170

However, Dr. Omar Abdel Rahman insisted on defending the cause of Islam during the trial even if this led to his conviction. Not only that, he put the judge in the dock, holding him responsible for the injustice which he might mete out on Muslims, warning him of God's wrath and punishment, and urging him to judge in accordance with the shari'ah.

Dr. Omar Abdel Rahman's opinion was that this was an opportunity that should not be missed to inform the regime of God's teachings. His testimony was the best defense he could offer to his brothers (co-defendants)--especially as the verdict was expected to be the death sentence--by showing the justness of their cause and their noble intention.

Indeed, the judge did not issue any death sentence in that case. He cited extenuating circumstances, such as the defendants' just cause and noble intention.

I cannot conclude the talk on Omar Abdel Rahman's statements at the trial without mentioning some of them which were strong in their justness and straightforwardness. This put him in a very difficult position because the prosecutor could have used these statements against him and demanded the death sentence for him. But he was the scholar of the mujahideen and the mujahid of the scholars.

Shaykh Omar said: The prosecutor says that those who raise the slogan that power is for God while they themselves want to monopolize power have been described by Muslims and Islamic history as "Khawarij" (old dissident sect of Islam). Yes, "power is for God" are words that were previously said by the noble son of Ishaq son of Ya'qub son of Ibrahim: the prophet of God, Yusuf, who said those words from his prison in Egypt.

The prison's restrictions did not prevent him from saying the words of truth, which were also said by other prophets. Therefore, this is the call of Muslims throughout history. The Khawarij said those words to the fourth orthodox caliph / If these words were said in the first age (of Islam), those who said them were Khawarij. If they were said in this age, those who said them are mujahideen."

Omar Abdel Rahman said this during the trial: The prosecutor's office has defended the sulh (conciliation) treaty between Egypt and Israel. I will not reply to the prosecutor's office. My reply to the committee formed by the Shaykh of Al-Azhar is enough. I will reply to the great scholar (sarcastically)--the prosecutor who testified that the treaty is valid on the basis of God's words: "As long as these stand true to you, stand ye to them," and "But if the enemy incline towards peace, do thou (also) incline towards peace." (Quranic verses) Did the Jews stand true to us? Did they incline towards peace."

Is it not we who inclined and stood true?

Omar Abdel Rahman also said: "My crime is that I have criticized the state and shown the corruption of the society and its hostility to God's religion. I have stood up everywhere saying the words of truth, which are the very basics of my religion and belief. My religion and conscience prompt me to fight injustice and tyranny, refute misconceptions and doubts, and expose the tyrants, even if this costs me my life and possessions."

I am not afraid of prison or execution. I am not happy if I am pardoned or acquitted. I am not sad if I am sentenced to death--it will be martyrdom for the sake of God. Then I will say: I have won, O God of the Kaaba. I am a Muslim who lives and dies for his religion. I cannot remain silent while Islam is being attacked everywhere.

In closing, Omar Abdel Rahman said: "O President of the Higher State Security Court: I have made my argument and said the truth. You must judge in accordance with the shari'ah and you must apply the rules of God. If you do not do this, you are an unbeliever, a wrongdoer, and a rebel."

> *By (the light of) what God hath revealed, they are (no better than) unbelievers.'*
>
> *By (the light of) what God hath revealed, they are (no better than) wrongdoers.*
>
> *By (the light of) what God hath revealed, they are those who rebel. (Koranic verses)*

O President of the Court: God prevents you from the government and the government does not prevent you from God (as published). God's orders are above everything else. There is no obedience in disobeying God's orders. I warn you of His wrath against criminal people.

As for the testimony of Shaykh Salah Abu-Isma'il (may God have mercy on him), it was serious because it contained clear answers to several serious questions pertaining to the regime in Egypt and its position on Islam.

Shaykh Salah Abu-Isma'il stressed that Anwar Al-Mujahideen, by saying that 'there was no politics in religion and no religion in politics,' had washed his hands of Islam.

In his testimony Shaykh Salah Abu-Isma'il explained his attempts to codify (Islamic) laws through the People's Assembly and his despair of the application of the shari'ah through this channel because of the government's maneuverings.

Those elections were a painful lesson to those who followed this course on the pretext that they would achieve the interest of Islam and establish a government ruled by the shari'ah. They claimed that the current circumstances required political flexibility in dealing with (religious) texts; they thus lost their religion but did not win the world. (reference to Muslim Brotherhood participation in the People's Assembly elections)

As for the court's sentences, they were a surprise to the government, the security services, and the prosecutor. The court did not issue any death sentences. It acquitted 194 out of 302 defendants.

The legal reasons on which the verdicts were based were more important than the verdicts:

- The court admitted that Egypt is not being governed in accordance with the Islamic shari'ah.

- The court admitted that a government that applies the shari'ah is a duty and a hope for every Muslim.

- The court admitted that the Egyptian Constitution and laws contravene the rules of Islam.

- The court admitted that many people have departed from Islam in the Egyptian society under the protection of the law.

- The court admitted that physical torture was used against the defendants, causing permanent disabilities to some of them. It demanded that those responsible for this torture be referred to investigation.

## Israel

The establishment of Israel has been a western objective for over two centuries. The Israeli presence in the region was considered a basic guarantee for serving the western interests. Israel separates between Egypt and Syria, the two regions that for several centuries served as a wall of steadfastness against the Crusades and the Tartar conquests and that continue to this day to constitute a considerable human weight in the heart of the Islamic world.

Let us remember Napoleon Bonaparte's statement to the Jews following his invasion of Egypt and his failure to conquer Akko in 1799. Remember Bonaparte's call to the Jews, whom he referred to as the "legitimate heirs to Palestine." Bonaparte's message to the Muslims and his flirtation with Islam was a brazen act of deception while his call to the Jews was a different case.

Anwar al-Mujahideen was not the first to sign a separate deal between Israel and the Arabs. Prince Faysal did that before him. The latter wanted to buy his kingdom from the British by selling Palestine to the Jews.

During the 1973 war, when the United States shipped weapons, ammunition, and tanks to Israel for 33 days, the goal was to compensate Israel for its war losses and to swiftly upgrade the combat capabilities. This is one of many examples about the US flagrant support for Israel, including the US pressure on Egypt to sign the Nuclear Nonproliferation Treaty at a time when Israel publicly declares that it will not sign the treaty because of its special circumstances. Despite this, the United States sympathizes with Israel and overlooks its actions. This means that the United States has deliberately left the nuclear weapons in the hands of Israel to threaten its Arab neighbors.

The western states tried for over two centuries to establish Israel. They considered its presence in the region a basic guarantee for serving the Western interests. Israel separates Egypt and Syria, the two major regions that for several years served as a wall of steadfastness against the Crusades and the Tartar conquests. Until this day they constitute a considerable human weight in the heart of the Islamic world.

As for France, it has tried since the end of the 18th Century to establish Israel. Here are some examples:

When Napoleon Bonaparte headed for Syria, following his invasion of Egypt, he failed to conquer Akko in 1799. As a result, he issued his famous call to the Jews everywhere. His statement was distributed in Palestine as well as simultaneously in France, Italy, the German provinces, and Spain. This indicates that the issue was far greater than a local incident that

Bonaparte faced, having failed to conquer the walls of Jerusalem. The statement said:

From Napoleon Bonaparte, the Supreme Commander of the Armed Forces in the French Republic in Africa and Asia, to the legitimate heirs of Palestine:

> *O Israelis; O unique people; the forces of conquest and tyranny have failed to deprive you of your origin and national existence, although they deprived you of the land of your ancestors."*

> *The neutral and rational observers of people's destiny, although they lacked the powers of prophets such as Isaiah and Joel, have realized the prophecies predicted by these prophets through their sublime faith; namely, that God's slaves (the word Israel in Hebrew means the slave of God) will return to Zion and chant. They will be overwhelmed with joy when they restore their kingdom without fear. Rise forcefully, O those expelled in the wilderness. You are facing a fierce battle waged by your people, after the enemy had considered the land inherited from the forefathers a booty to be divided among them as they wish.*

### Returning the "Pasha" to His Senses

At the end of 1838, Napoleon's conqueror and the commander of the British armies, Lord Willington, wrote a report to Lord Palmerston to give him a summary of the situation in the Near East.

A serious crisis broke out this year between Egypt and Turkey as a result of conflicts and contradictions caused by Egypt's wali (Ruler). In 10 years Muhammad Ali managed to build a fleet and an army that exceed the legitimate needs of his government. He has recruited 100,000 people and amassed them against his master, the Ottoman Caliph. These conditions require a swift action by the English Government as well as an urgent intervention that could bring the "Pasha", who imagines himself to be invincible, back to his senses, submission, and obedience of the Sultan."

It is worth noting here that Britain, one of the superpowers, has given itself the right to determine the legitimate defense needs of weaker governments. Whatever exceeds these needs is considered illegitimate. This is the same law that is being applied by the United States and major states against other countries. The United States and the major powers have the right to possess weapons of mass destruction while the weaker nations are denied this right.

The Jews took advantage of the complicated political circumstances at the time. Palmerston did not want the sick man (Turkey) to die before preparations are in place to divide his heritage. He also did not wish him to recover. Accordingly, it is necessary to establish a buffer zone that separates Egypt and Turkey. Each one must be kept in place and prevented from becoming stronger than necessary!

The quick and possible solution is to separate between the Ottoman Empire and the ambitions of Muhammad Ali and his allies. The Sultan and his entourage must realize that Muhammad Ali's ambitions are not confined to the Eastern Mediterranean only. They extend to the Red Sea and Aden to prove his control of the empire.

The buffer zone that could be thought of is the settlement of the Jews in Palestine. This would turn them into a thorn in the back of Muhammad Ali that would prevent him from threatening Turkey on one hand and stop him from having a free rein in the Red Sea as he wishes on the other hand.

Should the Sultan accept its advice, the British Government will be prepared to place the Jewish colonies in Palestine under its protection so that this could serve as a permanent warning to Muhammad Ali and deter him from threatening the supreme state.

In 1840, the European powers imposed two treaties on Muhammad Ali following his defeat. The first concerned him and his heirs who rule Egypt. The second was called the treaty of "easing the situation in Syria." On the surface, the second treaty secured the exit of Muhammad Ali's troops from Syria, but in actual fact it prepared the grounds for a massive Jewish immigration to Palestine and sought to achieve the basic demand related to the Ottoman Caliphate's heritage in the east, particularly the important strategic corner surrounding the Eastern Mediterranean, where Egypt and Syria are located.

In 1849, a small Jewish conference was held in London under the sponsorship of the Rothschild Family. The conference ended by making the following two demands:

1.  Declare the acceptance by the world Jews wherever they exist of the British protection.

2.  Appeal to the British Government to facilitate for the Jews the colonization of Palestine, as is the case in other regions.

In 1875 it came to British Prime Minister Disraeli's knowledge that Khedive Isma'il, the ruler of Egypt, wished to sell his shares in the Suez Canal Company.

Disraeli was the last Jewish Prime Minister in the history of England. If British politicians were driven by their Protestant religious feelings or political and military interests to seek the establishment of Israel, a Jewish politician such as Disraeli realized that such an atmosphere ought to be used to serve the sons of his religion. One of the main characters in a novel that he wrote early in his life said: England is too grand to be turned by some of its politicians into a large commercial accounting office. England has a heart and a conscience. Therefore, it stands alongside the Jews with the realization that God Himself is fighting for the resurrection of the Jews.

As soon as word of Khedive Isma'il's desire to sell his shares reached Disraeli, the latter realized that this was a golden opportunity for Britain to establish a foothold in Egypt in preparation for establishing Israel.

Disraeli had to think fast. The problem facing him was that the Khedive wanted the price in cash and the deal to be conducted in secrecy.

These two conditions prevented him from presenting the deal to parliament. He found a fast solution in the person of Baron Rothschild, who arranged for him next day 4 million gold pounds.

With England's purchase of Egypt's share in the Suez Canal, the events accelerated in favor of Israel.

In 1877, a little more than a year after the conclusion of the deal, the Rothschild family was financing the first settlement colony for the Jews in Palestine on an area of 2,275 feddans. It was the Pitah Tikfah settlement.

In the same year, the British Government asked the Sultan to permit the landing of military troops in Cyprus, noting that this was militarily necessary to monitor what goes on the Syrian coast following the English-Turkish (assistance) agreement concluded at the end of the Crimea war. Under this agreement, Britain promised the Sultan to protect his eastern property! In 1882, Britain cited the existence of disturbances in Egypt (Urabi's revolt) and made a decision to occupy Egypt and quell the Urabi revolution. Britain's excuse was that Urabi was rebelling against the Sultan. Thus, the troops of infidelity marched into the homes of Islam under the protection of the Sultan!

The Jewish immigration movement was much accelerated after the British occupation of Egypt. The number of settlement colonies mushroomed so much that 10 years after the British occupation of Egypt approximately 20 colonies were built. They ranged in area between 210 to 3,800 feddans west and east of the River Jordan.

At the start of the 20th Century, Word War I broke out. Before this war, the British policy knew exactly what it wanted in Palestine. This became clear in a recommendation made by British Prime Minister Campbell-Bannerman immediately before the war. It said verbatim: The establishment of an alien and strong human barrier on the bridge that connects Europe to the ancient world and links them to the Mediterranean and the Red Sea is a demand that must continue to guide us. It is imperative that we find the practical means for the implementation of this demand. This clearly meant an insistence to establish a Jewish state in Palestine.

During the war, the British Government, in 1915, asked Sir Herbert Samuel to outline a concept of what the situation in Palestine after the victory could be like.

Herbert Samuel, as a member of the War Ministry in addition to being a Jew and Zionist, wrote a memorandum on February 5, 1915 entitled the "Future of Palestine." The memorandum noted the following:

The solution that enjoys the greatest chance for success and guarantees the British interests is the establishment of a large Jewish federation under British mandate in Palestine. After the war, Palestine must be placed under British mandate.

In the spring of 1915, a few months after the start of the World War I, a person appeared in the scene of events who rendered invaluable services to the Jews. His name was Marx Sykes, who signed on behalf of Britain the famous Sykes-Picot Agreement, which blew the hopes of Britain's Arab allies up in the air along with the words of honor guaranteed by the British Crown.

The British documents reveal a dangerous idea that dominated the British policy during World War I and continued to dominate it for a long time thereafter. The core of this idea is that the holy sites of all religions in the Middle East must be placed under British control.

The British documents note that Musa Qatawi Pasha, head of the Jewish community in Egypt, asked General Maxwell, Commander-in-Chief of the British Forces in Egypt, in July 1916 for his permission to establish Jewish battalions within the General Allenby's army, which was getting ready to march against the Turks in Palestine and Syria. General Maxwell gave his permission and allowed troops from these battalions to place the Star of David at the front of their hats to make it clear that they belong to Jewish battalions.

In this atmosphere fraught with evil about carving up the heritage of the Ottoman State, hatred toward Islam, and blind fanaticism in favor of the Jews, the Balfour Declaration was issued on November 2, 1917. It said the following:

> *"His Majesty's Government view with favor the establishment in Palestine of a national home for the Jewish people, and will use their best endeavors to facilitate the achievement of this object."*

After the war and during the preparation of the peace documents at the peace conference in Versailles, the Zionist movement insisted on the need for the conference resolution on the British Mandate of Palestine to include a reference to the main task of the British mandate of Palestine; namely, to seek the establishment of a national home for the Jews.

In 1921 Lord Allenby, commander of the British troops that invaded Palestine and kicked the Turks out of it and later the British Commissioner in Egypt, asked Colonel Richard Meiner Tizhagen, Middle East Director of Operations, to draft a memorandum containing specific recommendations about Egypt and Palestine to submit to British Prime Minister Lloyd George.

We have to pause here. As is known, this is the policy being applied today regarding the disarmament of Sinai, which serves as a buffer zone between Egypt and Israel, under the Egyptian-Israeli peace treaty.

Britain's efforts did not stop at rendering services to the Jews militarily and politically. It put pressure on its Arab allies, who revolted in collaboration with the British against the Caliphate, to accept the existence eof Israel.

Upon the divulgence of the articles in the Sykes-Picot Agreement of 1917 and the Balfour Declaration that followed it, the Arab allies were greatly shocked. Britain sent Commander Hogarth, representing the Cairo Office, to meet with Al-Sharif Husayn in Jeddah to explain the circumstances and continue to put pressure on the subservient ally, who had no choice but to follow the line of subservience. The following is an excerpt from Commander Hogarth's report on the meeting:

> *"With respect to the Sykes-Picot, Al-Sharif Husayn said that if there is a marginal amendment to the original plans dictated by the war necessities he is prepared to acknowledge this necessity explicitly. However, he asked that we should inform him explicitly about the details of the required amendments and the necessities that dictate them."*

Al-Sharif Husayn raised the issue of France's demands in Syria. Commander Hogarth said: France now sees with our eyes (meaning the eyes of the English) as far as Syria is concerned. All that France wants is to protect and help Syria's independence. Al-Sharif Husayn did not seem convinced. Regarding the Balfour Declaration, Colonel Hogarth started to explain to Al-Sharif Husayn lengthy details about the growth of the Zionist movement during the war, the great value of the Jewish interests and Jewish influence, and the benefits of cooperating with them (meaning the Jewish, their interests, and their influence).

189

Al-Sharif Husayn's response indicated his willingness to accept the formula of the Balfour Declaration. In his report to the War Ministry in London, Colonel Hogarth said: Al-Sharif Husayn enthusiastically agreed and said that he welcomes the Jews in all the Arab countries.

As regards Prince Faysal, son of Al-Sharif Husayn, his mentor and famous British intelligence officers Lawrence convinced him to meet with Chaim Weizmann in Aqaba, in preparations for the Versailles Conference, in the first week of January 1919. The two signed an agreement that stipulated the following:

His Royal Highness Prince Faysal, representing and acting on behalf of the Arab Kingdom in Hijaz; and Dr. Chaim Weizmann, representing and acting on behalf of the Zionist movement, realize the closeness in race and ancient links between the Arabs and the Jewish people.

Based on the provisions of the agreement, we realize the following:

Faysal has recognized Palestine as a state on equal footing with the Hebrew State. He even recognized the final borders between the two sides.

Therefore, Anwar al-Mujahideen was not the first who signed a separate peace agreement between the Arabs and Israel.

The agreement also encouraged a large-scale Jewish immigration and recognized the Balfour Declaration.

## An Airlift Between the United States and Israel

The events and facts in this regard are too many to mention. Here are some important examples.

During the 1973 October war between the Arabs and Israel, the United States began airlifting to Israel weapons, ammunition, equipment, and even tanks from the warehouses of the operating US Army units directly into the battlefield.

Commenting on this airlift, former Egyptian War Minister Muhammad Abd-al-Ghani al-Jamasi says: The US airlift lasted for 33 days, from 13 October to 14 November 1973. Approximately 24 percent of the plane capacity of the Air Transport Command was used everyday throughout the period of the airlift.

Some 22,497 tons of weapons, equipment, and ammunition were airlifted to Israel, of which 39 percent was transported between 13-24 October 1973. Eight civilian Israeli 747s and 707s aircraft were used to transport 5,500 tons of equipment during the same period.

In addition to the airlift, 74 percent of the total magnitude of the urgent military plan for supplies and support was shipped by sea. The purpose of this operation was to compensate Israel for the war losses and expeditiously upgrade the combat capabilities.

The quality and quantity of the weapons, equipment, and ammunitions that reached Israel via the airlift were varied.

It is noticeable that the US airlift began on 13 October, the day that preceded the advanced Egyptian offensive toward the Sinai straits on 14 October. Israel managed to repulse this attack.

Through the airlift, the United States managed to upgrade the combat capabilities of the Israeli troops in the final stage of the October war.

This tipped the balance of military power in favor of Israel. It also demonstrated the US absolute support and backing for Israel in this war.

In my estimate, the US airlift and the US air reconnaissance flights over the Canal front on 13 and 15 October were the direct reason for causing an Israeli military superiority that enabled it to successfully carry out the Al-Difrswar Battle. Without this direct and flagrant military support for Israel, it would not have been able to achieve the success that it made in the last part of the war.

The political support for Israel, or the pressure exercised on its neighbors, have never ceased since its establishment. For example, on the same day the (Egyptian-Israeli) peace treaty was signed in Washington on March 26, 1979 the United States and Israel signed an agreement entitled "Agreement of Understanding Between the United States and Israel for Acknowledging Israel's Military Guarantees if the Egyptian-Israeli Peace Treaty is Violated."

The following are highlights from this dangerous agreement:

> *If it becomes known to the United States that a violation of the peace treaty, or a threat to violate it, has occurred, it will*

*consult with the parties on the measures that need to be adopted to end this violation.*

*It will adopt the measures it deems appropriate, including the diplomatic, economic, and military measures mentioned hereinafter.*

*The United States will adopt what it deems necessary to support the acts that Israel undertakes to confront such violations of the peace treaty, particularly if it is believed that the violation of the peace treaty threatens Israel's security. This includes, for instance, subjecting Israel to a blockade that prevents it from using international waterways, violating the peace treaty regarding troop limitations, or launching an armed attack on Israel. In such case, the United States is prepared to consider, with urgent speed, the adoption of such measures as beefing up the US presence in the region, supplying Israel with urgent needs, and exercising its maritime rights to put an end to this violation.*

*The United States will object to and necessarily reject any UN act or resolution that in its view runs contrary to the peace treaty!*

*The existing agreements or assurances
between the United States and Israel shall
not be revoked or amended by the peace
treaty!*

The United States handed a copy of this
memorandum to Al-Mujahideen a day before
the peace treaty was signed, but this did not
prevent Al-Mujahideen from signing the treaty
next day. He even signed a new document
entitled "A Complementary Agreement for Full
Autonomy in the West Bank and Gaza."

Upon examining this agreement, a number of
extremely serious meanings come to mind:

1. The United States has given itself the right to
use its military force against Egypt if the latter
undertakes an action that the United States
considers a violation of the peace treaty or a
threat to Israel's security.

2. The United States signed an agreement with
one side of the treaty, which is Israel, but not
with both sides. This means that any US threat
to use its influence and military power is
directed against Egypt only if it tries to violate
the treaty, but not against Israel.

3. The United States gave itself the right to object to any UN action or resolution that, in its views, conflicts with the peace treaty.

This means that the peace treaty and Israel's security are more important to the United States than the UN and its resolutions. This demonstrates the extent of US hypocrisy in using the UN and the international legitimacy to serve its interests.

The United States explicitly states its non-compliance with the UN resolutions as far as Israel's security is concerned. In the meantime, the poor countries in the world, particularly in the Israeli world, are committed to full compliance with the UN resolutions to the point of humiliation and the killing of hundreds of thousands of children.

4. According to the United States, this agreement is not revoked or amended by the peace treaty. This means that this agreement takes precedence over the peace treaty. However, Article 6 of the peace treaty between Egypt and Israel stipulates that "in the event the obligations of the parties under this treaty are in conflict with any other obligations the commitments arising from this treaty shall be binding and valid."

This means that the peace treaty takes precedence over any treaty that binds Egypt to declaring war against Israel. This limitation is intended to make Egypt give up its obligations under the common Arab Defense Pact. This pact binds Egypt to intervene against any aggression involving a member state of this pact.

The effect of this humiliating limitation was evident. After the peace treaty, Israel bombarded the nuclear reactor in Iraq, invaded southern Lebanon and placed an agent army there, occupied Dahlak island at the southern entrance to the Red Sea, increased its support for the secessionist movement in southern Sudan, and allied itself with Turkey to isolate Syria. It even suggested that Israel's security extends as far as Pakistan in the east, in a clear reference to the Pakistani nuclear program, which Israel considers a threat.

Among the flagrant examples that show the extent of the US support for Israel, to the point of forcing the regimes toward submission, is the US pressure on the Egyptian regime to sign the Nuclear Nonproliferation Treaty. Meanwhile, Israel publicly declares that it will not sign the treaty because of its special circumstances. Despite this, the United States declares its sympathy with Israel and overlooks its actions.

It is both astonishing and disturbing at the same time to see that a country such as Pakistan, which has strong ties with the United States, has refused to sign the treaty so long as its enemy India has not signed it. Unlike Egypt, Pakistan has not steeped down into the level to which the Egyptian regime reached in giving up everything to obey the United States.

It transpires from the above that the west has played a colluding role in establishing Israel in the heart of the Muslim nation. The US role in this crime was and remains one played by the leader of all criminals.

It also transpires that in playing this role, the western countries were backed by their peoples, who are free in their decision. It is true that they may be largely influenced by the media decision and distortion, but in the end they cast their votes in the elections to choose the governments that they want, pay taxes to fund their policy, and hold them accountable about how this money was spent.

Regardless of method by which these governments obtain the votes of the people, voters in the western countries ultimately cast their votes willingly. These peoples have willingly called for, supported, and backed the establishment of and survival of the State of Israel.

The western peoples continued to make this demand for decades, and it was not a haphazard demand. It was the fruit of a tree watered by hatred of Islam and the Muslims for several centuries. Based on this fact, we must build a realistic policy toward the west so that we do not fall from the sky of illusions to hit the land of reality.

In addition, we must acknowledge that the west, led by the United States, which is under the influence of the Jews, does not know the language of ethics, morality, and legitimate rights.

They only know the language of interests backed by brute military force. Therefore, if we wish to have a dialogue with them and make them aware of our rights, we must talk to them in the language that they understand.

### Egypt Has Restored Sinai Politically

Regarding the Egyptian-Israeli peace treaty, whoever examines the Egyptian-Israeli peace treaty will realize that it was intended to be a permanent treaty from which Egypt could not break loose.

It was concluded in an attempt to establish on the ground, by force and coercion, a situation whereby it would be difficult to change by any government hostile to Israel that comes after Al-Mujahideen.

## Killing Americans

Killing the Americans with a single bullet, a stab, or a device made up of a popular mixture or hitting them with an iron bar is not impossible. Likewise, burning their property with Molotov cocktail is not difficult.

Suicide operations are the most successful in inflicting damage on the opponent and the least costly in terms of casualties among the fundamentalists.

The targets and the type of weapons must be selected carefully to cause damage to the enemy's structure and deter it enough to make it stop its brutality.

Cause the greatest damage and inflict the maximum casualties on the opponent, no matter how much time and effort these operations take, because this is the language understood by the west.

The struggle for the establishment of the Muslim state cannot be considered a regional struggle, certainly not after it had been ascertained that the Crusader alliance led by the United States will not allow any Muslim force to reach power in the Arab countries.

Confining the battle to the domestic enemy, (within the Arab states), will not be feasible in this stage of the battle, which he considers the battle of every Muslim.

Victory by the armies cannot be achieved unless the infantry occupies the territory. Likewise, victory for the Islamic movements against the world alliance cannot be attained unless these movements possess an Islamic base in the heart of the Arab region.

Mobilizing and arming the nation will be up in the air, without any tangible results, until a fundamentalist state is established in the region.

The establishment of a Muslim state in the heart of the Islamic world is not an easy or close target. However, it is the hope of the Muslim nation to restore its fallen caliphate and regain its lost glory. Do not precipitate collision and to be patient about victory.

We must not despair of the repeated strikes and calamities. We must never lay down our arms no matter how much losses or sacrifices we endure. Let us start again after every strike, even if we had to begin from scratch.

If their plans are exposed, their members are arrested, and their existence is threatened, it is better for the movement to pull out whoever it could pull out quietly, without reluctance, hesitation, or reliance on illusions.

> *"And those who disbelieved said unto their messengers: Verily we will drive you out from our land, unless ye return to our religion. Then their lord inspired them, saying verily We shall destroy the wrongdoers. And verily We shall make you to swell in the land after them. This is for him who feareth My Majesty and feareth My threats." (Qu'ran)*

It's now time to explore the future of the jihad movement in Egypt in particular and the world in general.

**1. Emerging phenomena:**

Any neutral observer could discern a number of phenomena in our Islamic world in general and Egypt in particular:

**A. The universality of the battle:**

The western forces that are hostile to Islam have clearly identified their enemy. They refer to it as the Islamic fundamentalism. They are joined in this by their old enemy, Russia. They have adopted a number of tools to fight Islam, including:

1.      The United Nations.

2.      The friendly rulers of the Muslim peoples.

3.      The multinational corporations.

4.      The international communications and data exchange systems.

5.      The international news agencies and satellite media channels.

6.      The international relief agencies, which are being used as a cover for espionage, proselytizing, coup planning, and the transfer of weapons.

In the face of this alliance, a fundamentalist coalition is taking shape. It is made up of the jihad movements in the various lands of Islam as well as the two countries that have been liberated in the name of jihad for the sake of God (Afghanistan and Chechnya).

If this coalition is still at an early stage, its growth is increasingly and steadily accelerating.

It represents a growing power that is rallying under the banner of jihad for the sake of God and operating outside the scope of the new world order. It is free of the servitude for the dominating western empire. It promises destruction and ruin for the new Crusades against the lands of Islam. It is ready for revenge against the heads of the world's gathering of infidels, the United States, Russia, and Israel. It is anxious to seek retribution for the blood of the martyrs, the grief of the mothers, the deprivation of the orphans, the suffering of the detainees, and the sores of the tortured people throughout the land of Islam, from Eastern Turkestan to Andalusia (Islamic state in Spain).

This age is witnessing a new phenomenon that continues to gain ground. It is the phenomenon of the mujahid youths who have abandoned their families, country, wealth, studies, and jobs in search of jihad arenas for the sake of God.

## B. There is no solution without jihad:

With the emergence of this new batch of Islamists, who have been missing from the nation for a long time, a new awareness is increasingly developing among the sons of Islam, who are eager to uphold it; namely, that there is no solution without jihad.

The spread of this awareness has been augmented by the failure of all other methods that tried to evade assuming the burdens of jihad. The Algerian experience has provided a harsh lesson in this regard. It proved to Muslims that the west is not only an infidel but also a hypocrite and a liar. The principles that it brags about are exclusive to, and the personal property of, its people alone. They are not to be shared by the peoples of Islam, at least nothing more that what a master leaves his slave in terms of food crumbs.

The Islamic Salvation Front in Algeria has overlooked the tenets of the creed, the facts of history and politics, the balance of power, and the laws of control. It rushed to the ballot boxes in a bid to reach the presidential palaces and the ministries, only to find at the gates tanks loaded with French ammunition, with their barrels pointing at the chests of those who forgot the rules of confrontation between justice and falsehood. The guns of the Francophile officers brought them down to the land of reality from the skies of illusions.

The Islamic Salvation men thought that the gates of rule had been opened for them, but they were surprised to see themselves pushed toward the gates of detention camps and prisons and into the cells of the new world order.

Particularly helpful in reaching the conclusion that there is no solution without jihad were the brutality and arbitrary nature of the new Jewish Crusade that treats the Islamic nation with extreme contempt. As a result, the Muslims in general and the Arabs in particular are left with nothing that is dear to them. We have become like orphans in a banquet for the villains (Arabic proverb).

Someone may ask: Don't you think that you are contradicting yourself? A short while ago you talked about the spread of despair in the hearts of some leaders of the jihad movement and now you are talking about a widespread jihad awakening?

The answer is simple. All movements go through a cycle of erosion and renewal, but it is the ultimate result that determines the fate of a movement: Either extinction or growth.

## 2. Confirmed duties:

**A. The Islamic movement in general, and the jihad movements in particular, must train themselves** and their members on perseverance, patience, steadfastness, and adherence to firm principles. The leadership must set an example for the members to follow. This is the key to victory. "O ye who believe. Endure, outdo all others in endurance, be ready, and observe your duty to Allah, in order that ye may succeed." (Koranic verse)

If signs of relaxation and retreat start to show on the leadership, the movement must find ways to straighten out its leadership and not to permit it to deviate from the line of jihad.

The loyalty to the leadership and the acknowledgement of its precedence and merit represent a duty that must be emphasized and a value that must be consolidated. But if loyalty to the leadership reaches the point of declaring it holy and if the acknowledgement of its precedence and merit leads to infallibility, the movement will suffer from methodological blindness. Any leadership flaw could lead to a historic catastrophe, not only for the movement but also for the entire nation.

Hence comes the importance of the issue of leadership in Islamic action in general and jihad action in particular and the nation's need for a scientific, struggling, and rational leadership that could guide the nation, amidst the mighty storms and hurricanes, toward its goal with awareness and prudence, without losing sight of its path, stumbling aimlessly, or reversing its course.

### Mobilizing the Fundamentalist Movement

**B. The mobilization (tajyyish) of the nation, its participation in the struggle, and caution against the struggle of the elite with the authority:**

The jihad movement must come closer to the masses, defend their honor, fend off injustice, and lead them to the path of guidance and victory. It must step forward in the arena of sacrifice and excel to get its message across in a way that makes the right accessible to all seekers and that makes access to the origin and facts of religion simple and free of the complexities of terminology and the intricacies of composition.

The jihad movement must dedicate one of its wings to work with the masses, preach, provide services for the Muslim people, and share their concerns through all available avenues for charity and educational work. We must not leave a single area unoccupied. We must win the people's confidence, respect, and affection. The people will not love us unless they felt that we love them, care about them, and are ready to defend them.

In short, in waging the battle the jihad movement must be in the middle, or ahead, of the nation. It must be extremely careful not to get isolated from its nation or engage the government in the battle of the elite against the authority.

We must not blame the nation for not responding or not living up to the task. Instead, we must blame ourselves for failing to deliver the message, show compassion, and sacrifice.

The jihad movement must be eager to make room for the Muslim nation to participate with it in the jihad for the sake of empowerment (al-tamkin). The Muslim nation will not participate with it unless the slogans of the mujahideen are understood by the masses of the Muslim nation.

The one slogan that has been well understood by the nation and to which it has been responding for the past 50 years is the call for the jihad against Israel. In addition to this slogan, the nation in this decade is geared against the US presence. It has responded favorably to the call for the jihad against the Americans.

A single look at the history of the mujahideen in Afghanistan, Palestine, and Chechnya will show that the jihad movement has moved to the center of the leadership of the nation when it adopted the slogan of liberating the nation from its external enemies and when it portrayed it as a battle of Islam against infidelity and infidels.

The strange thing is that secularists, who brought disasters to the Muslim nation, particularly on the arena of the Arab-Israeli conflict; and who started the march of treason by recognizing Israel beginning with the Armistice Agreement of 1949, as we explained earlier, are the ones who talk the most about the issue of Palestine.

Stranger still is the fact that the Muslims, who have sacrificed the most for Jerusalem, whose doctrine and Shari'ah prevent them from abandoning any part of Palestine or recognizing Israel, as we explained earlier; and who are the most capable of leading the nation in its jihad against Israel are the least active in championing the issue of Palestine and raising its slogans among the masses.

The jihad movement's opportunity to lead the nation toward jihad to liberate Palestine is now doubled. All the secular currents that paid lip service to the issue of Palestine and competed with the Islamic movement to lead the nation in this regard are now exposed before the Muslim nation following their recognition of Israel's existence and adoption of negotiations and compliance with the international resolutions to liberate what is left, or permitted by Israel, of Palestine. These currents differ among themselves on the amount of crumbs thrown by Israel to the Muslim and the Arabs.

The fact that must be acknowledged is that the issue of Palestine is the cause that has been firing up the feelings of the Muslim nation from Morocco to Indonesia for the past 50 years. In addition, it is a rallying point for all the Arabs, be they believers or non-believers, good or evil.

## Small Groups Could
## Frighten the Americans

Through this jihad the stances of the rulers, their henchmen of ulema of the sultan (reference to pro-government clerics), writers, and judges, and the security agencies will be exposed.

By so doing, the Islamic movement will prove their treason before the masses of the Muslim nation and demonstrate that the reason for their treason is a flaw in their faith. They have allied themselves with the enemies of God against His supporters and antagonized the mujahideen, because of their Islam and jihad, in favor of the Jewish and Christian enemies of the nation. They have committed a violation of monotheism by supporting the infidels against the Muslims.

Tracking down the Americans and the Jews is not impossible. Killing them with a single bullet, a stab, or a device made up of a popular mix of explosives or hitting them with an iron rod is not impossible. Burning down their property with Molotov Cocktails is not difficult. With the available means, small groups could prove to be a frightening horror for the Americans and the Jews.

**C. The Islamic movement in general and the jihad movement in particular must launch a battle for orienting the nation by:**

- Exposing the rulers who are fighting Islam.

- Highlighting the importance of loyalty to the faithful and relinquishment of the infidels in the Muslim creed.

- Holding every Muslim responsible for defending Islam, its sanctities, nation, and homeland.

- Cautioning against the ulema of the sultan and reminding the nation of the virtues of the ulema of jihad and the imams of sacrifice and the need for the nation to defend, protect, honor, and follow them.

- Exposing the extent of aggression against our creed and sanctities and the plundering of our wealth.

**D. Adherence to the goal of establishing the Muslim state in the heart of the Islamic world:**

The jihad movement must adopt its plan on the basis of controlling a piece of land in the heart of the Islamic world on which it could establish and protect the state of Islam and launch its battle to restore the rational caliphate based on the traditions of the prophet.

### Toward a Fundamentalist Base in the Heart of the Islamic World

Armies achieve victory only when the infantry takes hold of land. Likewise, the mujahid Islamic movement will not triumph against the world coalition unless it possesses a fundamentalist base in the heart of the Islamic world. All the means and plans that we have reviewed for mobilizing the nation will remain up in the air without a tangible gain or benefit unless they lead to the establishment of the state of caliphate in the heart of the Islamic world.

Nur-al-Din Zanki, and Salah-al-Din al-Ayyubi (Saladin) after him, may God bless their souls, have fought scores of battles until Nur-al-Din managed to wrestle Damascus from of the hands of the hypocrites and unified Greater Syria under his command. He sent Salah-al-Din to Egypt, where he fought one battle after another until he brought Egypt under his control. When Egypt and Syria were unified after the death of Nur-al-Din, the mujahid Sultan Salah-al-Din managed to win the battle of Hittin and conquered Bayt al-Maqdis (Islamic name for Jerusalem). Only then did the cycle of history turn against the Crusaders.

If the successful operations against Islam's enemies and the severe damage inflicted on them do not serve the ultimate goal of establishing the Muslim nation in the heart of the Islamic world, they will be nothing more than disturbing acts, regardless of their magnitude, that could be absorbed and endured, even if after some time and with some losses.

The establishment of a Muslim state in the heart of the Islamic world is not an easy goal or an objective that is close at hand. But it constitutes the hope of the Muslim nation to reinstate its fallen caliphate and regain its lost glory.

**E. If the goal of the jihad movement in the heart of the Islamic world in general and Egypt in particular is to cause change and establish an Islamic state, it must not precipitate collision or be impatient about victory.**

The jihad movement must patiently build its structure until it is well established. It must pool enough resources and supporters and devise enough plans to fight the battle at the time and arena that it chooses.

However, an extremely important and serious question arises here; namely, what if the movement's members or plans are uncovered, if its members are arrested, the movement's survival is at risk, and a campaign of arrests and storming operations targets its members, funds, resources, and leaders?

In this case, the movement must ask itself a specific question and give a clear answer.

Could it disperse in the face of the storm and pull out of the field with the least possible casualties? Or is patience not feasible and means total defeat and there is no room for withdrawal?

Or perhaps the answer could be a combination of the two aforesaid scenarios, meaning that it could pull out some of its leaders and members safely, leaving some others to face the risk of captivity and brutality.

In my opinion, the answer is that the movement must pull out as many personnel as possible to the safety of a shelter without hesitation, reluctance, or reliance on illusions. The most serious decision facing someone under siege is the escape decision. It is the hardest thing to leave the family, the position, the job, and the steady style of life and proceed to the unknown, uncertainties, and the uneasy life.

But as soon as the door of the cell closes behind the prisoner he wishes that he had spent his entire life displaced without a shelter rather than facing the humiliating experience of captivity.

But if the entire movement, or part of it, faces a situation where the noose is being tightened around it and its collapse is a matter of days or hours, the movement, or at least this wing of the movement, must initiate the battle of collision with the regime so that nobody is captured or killed for nothing.

Here, we must recall what we have already explained in terms of the nature of the composition of the universal regime that is hostile to Islam and its relationship with the ruling regimes in our countries. As we emphasized earlier, we must mobilize the nation in the battle of Islam against infidelity. We cautioned earlier against the risk of seeing the Muslim vanguards getting killed in silence as part of the battle of the elite against the authority.

## Striking at the Americans and the Jews

Thus, if the unjust forces drag us into a battle at a time that we do not want, we must respond in the arena that we choose; namely, to strike at the Americans and the Jews in our countries. By this, we win three times:

First, by dealing the blow to the great master, which is hiding from our strikes behind its agent.

Second, by winning over the nation when we choose a target that it favors, one that it sympathizes with those who hit it.

Third, by exposing the regime before the Muslim people when this regime attacks us to defend its US and Jewish masters, thus showing its ugly face, the face of the hired policeman who is faithfully serving the occupiers and the enemies of the Muslim nation.

**F. It is a long road of jihad and sacrifice**. If our goal is comprehensive change and if our path, as the Koran and our history have shown us, is a long road of jihad and sacrifices, we must not despair of repeated strikes and recurring calamities. We must never lay down our arms, regardless of the casualties or sacrifices.

We must realize that countries do not fall all of a sudden. They fall by pushing and overcoming.

### Moving the Battle to the Enemy

**G. The Islamic movement and its jihad vanguards, and actually the entire Islamic nation, must involve the major criminals.** This includes the United States, Russia, and Israel-in the battle and do not let them run the battle between the jihad movement and our governments in safety. They must pay the price, and pay dearly for that matter.

The masters in Washington and Tel Aviv are using the regimes to protect their interests and to fight the battle against the Muslims on their behalf. If the shrapnel from the battle reach their homes and bodies, they will trade accusations with their agents about who is responsible for this. In that case, they will face one of two bitter choices: Either personally wage the battle against the Muslims, which means that the battle will turn into clear-cut jihad against infidels, or they reconsider their plans after acknowledging the failure of the brute and violent confrontation against Muslims.

Therefore, we must move the battle to the enemy's grounds to burn the hands of those who ignite fire in our countries.

**H. The struggle for the establishment of the Muslim state cannot be launched as a regional struggle:**

It is clear from the above that the Jewish-Crusade alliance, led by the United States, will not allow any Muslim force to reach power in any of the Islamic countries. It will mobilize all its power to hit it and remove it from power. Toward that end, it will open a battlefront against it that includes the entire world. It will impose sanctions on whoever helps it, if it does not declare war against them altogether. Therefore, to adjust to this new reality we must prepare ourselves for a battle that is not confined to a single region, one that includes the apostate domestic enemy and the Jewish-Crusade external enemy.

**I. The struggle against the external enemy cannot be postponed:**

It is clear from the above that the Jewish-Crusade alliance will not give us time to defeat the domestic enemy then declare war against it thereafter. The Americans, the Jews, and their allies are present now with their forces, as we explained before.

**J. Unity before the single enemy:**

The jihad movement must realize that half the road to victory is attained through its unity, rise above trivial matters, gratitude, and glorification of the interests of Islam above personal whims.

The importance of the unity of the mujahid Islamic movement is perhaps clear now more than anytime before. The movement must seek this unity as soon as possible if it is serious in its quest for victory.

**K. Rallying around and supporting the struggling countries:**

Backing and supporting Afghanistan and Chechnya and defending them with the heart, the hand, and the word represent a current duty, for these are the assets of Islam in this age. The Jewish-Crusade campaign is united to crush them. Therefore, we must not be content with safeguarding them only. We must seek to move the battlefront to the heart of the Islamic world, which represents the true arena of the battle and the theatre of the major battles in defense of Islam.

In this regard, these two steadfast castles my not help us much because of many circumstances, the tremendous pressure, and the apparent weakness. Therefore, we must solve this problem ourselves without exposing them to pressure and strikes. This could pose a dilemma for the jihad movement, but it is not impossible to handle. It may be difficult, but it is possible, God willing. "And whosoever keepeth his duty to Allah, Allah will appoint a way out for him." (Koranic verse)

## Choosing the Targets and Concentrating on the Martyrdom Operations

### L. Changing the method of strikes:

The mujahid Islamic movement must escalate its methods of strikes and tools of resisting the enemies to keep up with the tremendous increase in the number of its enemies, the quality of their weapons, their destructive powers, their disregard for all taboos, and disrespect for the customs of wars and conflicts. In this regard, we concentrate on the following:

1. The need to inflict the maximum casualties against the opponent, for this is the language understood by the west, no matter how much time and effort such operations take.

2. The need to concentrate on the method of martyrdom operations as the most successful way of inflicting damage against the opponent and the least costly to the mujahideen in terms of casualties.

3. The targets as well as the type and method of weapons used must be chosen to have an impact on the structure of the enemy and deter it enough to stop its brutality, arrogance, and disregard for all taboos and customs. It must restore the struggle to its real size.

4. To reemphasize what we have already explained, we reiterate that focusing on the domestic enemy alone will not be feasible at this stage.

**M. The battle is for every Muslim**

An important point that must be underlined is that this battle, which we must wage to defend our creed, Muslim nation, sanctities, honor, values, wealth, and power, is a battle facing every Muslim, young or old.

It is a battle that is broad enough to affect every one of us at home, work, in his children, or dignity.

In order for the masses to move, they need the following:

1. A leadership that they could trust, follow, and understand.

2. A clear enemy to strike at.

3. The shackles of fear and the impediments of weakness in the souls must be broken.

These needs demonstrate to us the serious effects of the so-called initiative to end the violence and similar calls that seek to distort the image of the leadership and take the nation back to the prison of weakness and fear.

To illustrate this danger, let us ask ourselves this question: What will we tell the future generations about our achievements?

Are we going to tell them that we carried arms against our enemies then dropped them and asked them to accept our surrender?

## N. What jihad value could the future generation benefit from such conduct?

We must get our message across to the masses of the nation and break the media siege imposed on the jihad movement. This is an independent battle that we must launch side by side with the military battle.

Liberating the Muslim nation, confronting the enemies of Islam, and launching jihad against them require a Muslim authority, established on a Muslim land, that raises the banner of jihad and rallies the Muslims around it. Without achieving this goal our actions will mean nothing more than mere and repeated disturbances that will not lead to the aspired goal, which is the restoration of the caliphate and the dismissal of the invaders from the land of Islam.

This goal must remain the basic objective of the Islamic jihad movement, regardless of the sacrifices and the time involved.

# Part II

# Selected Communiques and Messages from Dr. Ayman al Zawahiri released after the September 11, 2001 Attacks

**By Dr. Ayman al Zawahiri**
*(translation by Laura Mansfield)*

# Selected Communiques and Messages from Dr. Ayman al Zawahiri released after the September 11, 2001 Attacks

### By Dr. Ayman al Zawahiri
### *(translation by Laura Mansfield)*

*By Laura Mansfield*

## September 9, 2004
## Dr. Ayman al-Zawahiri
## "The Defeat of America is a Matter of Time"

The mujahedeen fighters in Iraq turned America's plan upside down.

The defeat of America in Iraq and Afghanistan has become just a matter of time, with God's help," he said.

Americans in both countries are between two fires. If they carry on, they will bleed to death -- and if they pull out, they lose everything.

American forces are hunkered down and afraid to respond to advances of the mujahedeen.

East and south Afghanistan is an open battlefield for the mujahedeen, while the liars are hiding in the big capitals.

The Americans are hiding now in trenches and they refuse to come out and meet the mujahedeen, despite the mujahedeen antagonizing them with bombing and shooting and roadblocks around them. Their defense focuses on airstrikes, which wastes America's money in just stirring up sand.

## Oct. 1, 2004
## Dr. Ayman al-Zawahiri
## Muslim Youth: Do Not Wait

Defending Palestine is a responsibility for all Muslims. You should never give up Palestine even if the whole world drops it. In Palestine we don't face the Jews only, but the anti-Muslim world coalition led by America the Crusader and the Zionist. We know who killed Ahmad Yassin and Rantissi, it wasn't Israel alone that killed them. The U.S. and Europe and our leaders supported them in their act.

This is the century of the Islamic resistance after the governments have weakened and kneeled down before the invading crusader.

Let's learn a lesson from Chechnya, Afghanistan, Iraq, Palestine where the authority has vanished or was removed from power but the resistance remained. The governments in Chechnya and Afghanistan were transformed into resistance leadership.

We shouldn't wait for the American, English, French, Jewish, Hungarian, Polish and South Korean forces to invade Egypt, the Arabian Peninsula, Yemen and Algeria and then start the resistance after the occupier had already invaded us. We should start now.

The interests of America, Britain, Australia, France, Norway, Poland, South Korea and Japan are everywhere. All of them were a part of the invasion of Afghanistan, Iraq and Chechnya, they also enabled Israel.

We cannot not wait anymore than we have already or else we will be devoured one country at a time as they have occupied us in the last two centuries. The Islamic world has entered the period of occupation and division. The resistance foiled the crusaders' and Jews' plans and put them in an embarrassing defensive and they're looking for a way out.

If the mujahideen acted like cowards in Iraq, Afghanistan, Chechnya and Palestine, the enemy would have taken control of those countries. The people of experience and wisdom should gather forces to create a leadership for the resistance to face the crusaders' campaign as the mujahideen had done in Afghanistan and Chechnya against the will of the occupier and the agent government.

Oh young men of Islam, here is our message to you, if we are killed or captured, you should carry on the fight.

## November 29, 2004
## Dr. Ayman al Zawahiri
## "Policies must change no matter who wins"

*Translator's note:* In this video tape, Dr. Ayman al-Zawahiri warns that America must change its policies toward the Muslim world, no matter who is elected president.

These days, the U.S. is playing the election game in America, Afghanistan, and Iraq. As for the U.S. elections, the two candidates compete over placating Israel. That is, they compete over the crime against the Muslim nation that has been going on in Palestine for 87 years. This proves that there is no solution with America except to forcefully make it submit to justice.

Ahmad Shawqi said: 'If you counter evil with goodness you cannot defeat it, when you counter evil with evil, it will be cut off.'

We say to the American nation: 'Elect whoever you want, Bush, Kerry, or Satan himself.' We don't care. We care about purifying our country of the aggressors and resisting anyone who attacks us, violates our holy places, or steals our resources.

Here is a piece of advice for America that I must offer, even though I know they won't listen: You must choose one of two paths in your treatment of the Muslims.

Either you treat them either with respect, or as if our lives and property are available for you to invade, and as holy places to be desecrated. This is your problem, and you must make your own choice.

You must know that we are a nation of endurance and perseverance, and, Allah willing, we will remain steadfast, fighting you until Judgment Day.

In order to be a nation graced with endurance and perseverance, we must understand a number of important facts: The first is that the fall of Baghdad is, in fact, the fall of all the regimes that relinquished Jihad and assisted the invasion of Iraq. Even those that did not fall publicly fell long ago, with no noise, clatter of guns, or bombardment. Those not captured by the Crusading forces today are expected to become their targets tomorrow.

The second fact is that Baghdad was not occupied on April 9, 2003. It fell long before. It fell when Khedive Tawfiq sought the help of the British to restore him to the throne of Egypt in exchange for Egypt's occupation; when Sharif Hussein agreed with the British on a rebellion against the country of the Caliphate or when Abdel Aziz Al Saud agreed to be under American protection, British authority and later American; and when the Arabs accepted the peace agreement in 1949. Afterwards, the Arabs continued to deteriorate from one agreement to the other, until Oslo and the Quartet's road map.

## February 5, 2005
## Dr. Ayman al-Zawahiri
## Horreya (Freedom)

*Translator's Note: On Tuesday, 1 February 2005, a written statement said to be the transcript of an audio taped recording of a speech purportedly by al Qaeda second in command Ayman al-Zawahri first appeared on several Islamist Internet sites. The posting of the transcript was followed by the audio, and finally, a two-part flash presentation produced by al Qaeda's media outlet Sahab Enterprises. The title of the presentation is "Horreya," or "Freedom" as translated from Arabic into English. The overall theme and message focuses on the steps that must be followed in order for the Islamic world to be set free from non-Islamic oppression.*

America has for some time sought to establish the presence of its Crusade military in the Islamic world... And the way in which they will establish this presence is through their support of the Zionist entity, which is the main springboard for the Crusader invasion of the Islamic world. Therefore the consideration of the Jewish occupation of Palestine as a restricted regional case in Palestine alone, affecting only the Palestinians, is not possible.

And with the arrival of the current administration in the White House, the envious Crusader ambitions reached the peak of its foolishness in the support of Israel. They were not expecting what they face - thank God - with this great Islamic resistance, in return for its arrogance and its tyranny, that resistance, which reached its peak with the two blessed battles of New York and Washington.

The blind bull, America, decided to invade Afghanistan. Then its foolishness increased and they decided to invade Iraq. Then America discovered that it is up to their ears in the greatest trouble that they have faced in their history.

They have watched how the Soviet Union disintegrated and lost its influence after its withdrawal in defeat from Afghanistan, after they[the Soviet Union] accepted their defeat in a war of attrition that squandered their resources without accomplishing their goal: the extension of the realm of influence.

Instead the reverse happened – in less than two years – as they know well in the Soviet Union.

The freedom that we want is not the freedom of lowly rascal America. It is not the freedom of the usurious banks and the giant companies and the misleading Mass Media Organizations. It is not the freedom to ruin others for the sake of one's own material interests. It is not the freedom of AIDS and the industry of atrocities and same-sex marriage. It is not the freedom of gambling and wine and the breakdown of the family, and the freedom for women to be used as a commodity for bringing in customers and signing deals, and attacking passengers, and selling goods. . It is not the freedom of two-faced principles and the division of the people into looters and looted. It is not the freedom of Hiroshima and Nagasaki.

It is not the freedom trading torture systems, and of supporting the systems used to defeat and suppress others at the hands of America's friends. It is not the freedom of Israel in the extermination of the Muslims and the destruction of the Al Aqsa Mosque and the Judaization of Palestine.

It is not the freedom of Guantanamo and Abu Ghareb. It is not the freedom of the bombing of Al Sagadi, with seven ton bombs and cluster bombs, and dropping leaflets and depleted uranium, and destroying the villages of Afghanistan and Iraq. It is not the blood suckers or the freedom that comes from the monopoly of weapons of mass destruction, and prohibiting others from developing them. It is not the freedom of decision of those in the monopoly of the International Community, where four of the five senior members are Crusaders.

Our freedom is the freedom of unity and manners and chastity and fairness and justice.

And therefore, any reform that seeks that freedom depends on three things:

- Rule of the Qu'ran
- Liberation of the homelands
- Liberation of the people

They will be come about except through jihad, and struggle, and more struggle, and martyrdom. They will not come about unless we eject the enemies from our homes, and seize our rights with the power of jihad. The enemies will not leave our homes if we show kindness or ask them.

And in this greatest battle the role of our young men has become clear taking into consideration that their leadership in battle has spoiled – thank God – the plans of the Crusaders and the Jews in Afghanistan and Iraq and Palestine and Chechnya.

The Muslim young men must spread this battle against the Jews and the Crusaders as far as possible on the earth, and they must threaten their interests everywhere, and not allow them rest or stability.
In this, the greatest battle, the role of money is confirmed as the nerve center of the war, and as its fuel. Therefore we should offer our financial Zakat to the militants and to the support of the battle against the Crusaders and

the Jews. We should avoid by every means possible the payment of taxes and fees to the collaborating governments, who will use these funds for the execution of the policies of the Crusaders and the Jews.

And in this, the greatest battle, it becomes clear that the teachers and the educators and the professors and journalists and the unions, and the tribal sheikhs, and merchants, and all segments of the community without exception must join in.

And in this, the greatest battle, the men of thought and command must be united for the national interest under the flag of Jihad for Allah, and must organize the resistance, and delegate the responsibilities, and consolidate the power.

And in this, the greatest battle, it is necessary for us all, both individuals and groups and organizations, that we unite together for the sake of jihad against the Crusaders and Jews, and their judgmental agents in our lands, and that we do not accept any compromise with them, nor any plan that offer that gives them legitimacy and justifies their actions. We must challenge them and antagonize then, and incite their hatred, and gather the nation together to fight against them.

O you, the Muslims, join in the fight for the sake of Allah, and under our slogan: "the liberation of the people and their homelands under the banner of the Qu'ran

And our closing prayer is praise to Allah, the Lord of the Worlds, and we invoke the peace of Allah and his blessings upon our master Mohamed and his family and his friends.

## February 21, 2005
## Ayman al-Zawahiri

Today, Three years have gone by since the first group of Muslim prisoners were sent to the Guantanamo prison camp after thousands were betrayed in Mazar el Sharif [Afghanistan] by the unbelievers.

One may ask why all this interest in Guantanamo when our countries are filled with a thousand Guantanamos under U.S. observation.

The reform which emerges from U.S. prisons like Bagram, Kandahar, Guantanamo, Abu Ghraib, and from the launch of cluster bombs and rockets and the appointment of the likes of Karzai and Allawi.

It is because Guantanamo exposes the truth of reform and democracy that America claims it aims to spread in our countries.

If you, the people of the West, think that these cardboard governments can protect you, you are wrong.

Real security is based on mutual cooperation with the Islamic nation on the basis of mutual respect and the stopping of aggression

Your new crusade will, God willing, be defeated in the end, just like your earlier ones. But this will not happen, however, until after tens of thousands of your people are killed, and your economy is ruined, and after your actions have been exposed on the pages of history.

## June 18, 2005
## Dr. Ayman al-Zawahiri
## True Reform is Only Through Jihad

*Translator's note:* *This video was released on June 17, 2005, on Al Jazeera, and then subsequently on the internet.*

True reform is based on three principles:

The first principle is the rule of Sharia because Sharia, was given by God, and protects the believers' interests, freedom, honor, and pride, and protects what is sacred to them. The Islamic nation will not accept any other law, after it has suffered from the anti-Islamic trends forcefully imposed on it.

The second principle of reform is the freedom of the lands of Islam. No reform is conceivable while our countries are occupied by the Crusader forces, which are spread throughout our countries. No reform is conceivable while the Crusader forces are stationed in our countries [where they] enjoy support, supplies, and storage facilities, and go forth from our countries to attack our brothers and sisters in other Islamic countries. No reform is conceivable while our governments are controlled by the American embassies, which stick their noses into all our affairs.

The third principle of reform is the Muslim nation's freedom to run its own affairs. This reform will only be realized in two ways. First, freedom of the independent religious judicial system, the implementation of its rulings, and the guaranteeing of its honor, authority, and strength. Second, the freedom and the right of the Islamic nation to implement the principle of 'promoting virtue and preventing vice.'

Driving out the invading crusader forces and Jews from our Muslim homes cannot be realized solely through demonstrations and speaking out in the streets. Reform and expelling the invaders from Muslim countries cannot be accomplished except by fighting for the sake of God.

Allah said: 'Fight them until all strife ceases and religion is professed for the pleasure of Allah alone.' He also said: 'Fight them, and Allah will punish them at your hands and will humiliate them, and will help you to overcome them, and will relieve the minds of the believers.'

I salute my brothers, the lions of Islam, who are on the holy front of Islam around Jerusalem. I call upon them in the name of Allah not to abandon their Jihad, not to throw down their weapons, not to believe the counsel of the collaborators, not to forget the lessons of history, not to trust the secularists who have sold Palestine cheaply, and not to be drawn into the secular game of elections in accordance with a secular constitution.

## Letter from al-Zawahiri to al-Zarqawi

## October 11, 2005

In the name of God, praise be to God, and praise and blessings be upon the Messenger of

God, his family, his Companions, and all those who follow him.

The gracious brother/Abu Musab, God protect him and watch over him, may His religion, and His Book and the Sunna of His Prophet aid him, I ask the Almighty that he bless him, us, and all Muslims, with His divine aid, His clear victory, and His release from suffering be close at hand. Likewise, I ask the Almighty to gather us as He sees fit from the glory of this world and the prize of the hereafter.

1. Dear brother, God Almighty knows how much I miss meeting with you, how much I long to join you in your historic battle against the greatest of criminals and apostates in the heart of the Islamic world, the field where epic and major battles in the history of Islam were fought. I think that if I could find a way to you, I would not delay a day, God willing.

2. My dear brother, we are following your news, despite the difficulty and hardship. We

received your last published message sent to Sheikh Usama Bin Ladin, God save him. Likewise, I made sure in my last speech that Aljazeera broadcast Saturday, 11 Jumadi I, 1426 AH (June 18, 2005) to mention you, send you greetings, and show support and thanks for the heroic acts you are performing in defense of Islam and the Muslims, but I do not know what Al Jazeera broadcast. Did this part appear or not? I will try to attach the full speech with this message, conditions permitting.

Likewise, I showed my support for your noble initiative to join with your brothers, during a prior speech I sent to the brothers a number of months ago, but the brothers' circumstances prevented its publication.

3.    I want to reassure you about our situation. The summer started hot with operations escalating in Afghanistan. The enemy struck a blow against us with the arrest of Abu al-Faraj, may God break his bonds. However, no Arab brother was arrested because of him. The brothers tried - and were successful to a great degree - to contain the fall of Abu al-Faraj as much as they could.

However, the real danger comes from the agent Pakistani army that is carrying out operations in the tribal areas looking for mujahideen.

4.    I want to keep corresponding with you about the details of what is going on in dear Iraq, especially since we do not know the full truth as you know it.  Therefore, I want  you to explain to me your situation in a little detail, especially in regards to the political angle.  I want you to express to me what is on your mind in regards to what is on my mind in the way of questions and inquiries.

A.    I want to be the first to congratulate you for what God has blessed you with in terms  of fighting battle in the heart of the Islamic world, which was formerly the field for major battles in Islam's history, and what is now the place for the greatest battle of  Islam in this era, and what will happen, according to what appeared in the Hadiths of the Messenger of God about the epic battles between Islam and atheism.

It has always been my belief that the victory of Islam will never take place until a Muslim state is established in the manner of the Prophet in the heart of the Islamic world, specifically in the Levant, Egypt, and the neighboring states of the Peninsula and Iraq; however, the center would be in the Levant and Egypt.  This is my opinion, which I do not preach as infallible, but I  have  reviewed  historical  events  and  the behavior of the enemies of Islam themselves, and they did not establish Israel in this triangle surrounded by Egypt and Syria and overlooking the Hijaz except for their own interests.

As for the battles that are going on in the far-flung regions of the Islamic world, such as Chechnya, Afghanistan, Kashmir, and Bosnia, they are just the groundwork and the vanguard for the major battles which have begun in the heart of the Islamic world. We ask God that He send down his victory upon us that he promised to his faithful worshippers.

It is strange that the Arab nationalists also have, despite their avoidance of Islamic practice, come to comprehend the great importance of this province. It is like a bird whose wings are Egypt and Syria, and whose heart is Palestine. They have come to comprehend the goal of planting Israel in this region, and they are not misled in this, rather they have admitted their ignorance of the religious nature of this conflict.

What I mean is that God has blessed you and your brothers while many of the Muslim mujahideen have longed for that blessing, and that is Jihad in the heart of the Islamic world. He has, in addition to that, granted you superiority over the idolatrous infidels, traitorous apostates, and those turncoat deviants.

This is what God Almighty has distinguished you and your brothers with over the mujahedeen before you who fought in the heart of the Islamic world, and in Egypt and Syria to be precise, but this splendor and superiority against the enemies of Islam was not ordained for them.

God also blessed you not only with the splendor of the spearhead of Jihad, but with the splendor as well of the doctrines of monotheism, the rejection of polytheism, and avoidance of the tenets of the secularists and detractors and inferiors, the call to the pure way of the Prophet, and the sublime goal that the Prophet left to his companions. This is a blessing on top of blessing on top of blessing which obliges you and your noble brothers to be constantly thankful and full of praise. The Almighty said: *If ye are grateful, He is pleased with you* and the Almighty says: *If ye are grateful, I will add more unto you.*

B. Because of this, we are extremely concerned, as are the mujahideen and all sincere Muslims, about your Jihad and your heroic acts until you reach its intended goal.

You know well that purity of faith and the correct way of living are not connected necessarily to success in the field unless you take into consideration the reasons and practices which events are guided by. For the grandson of the Prophet Imam al Hussein Bin Ali, the Leader of the Faithful Abdallah Bin al-Zubair, Abdul Rahman Bin al-Ashath, and other great people, did not achieve their sought-after goal.

C.  If our intended goal in this age is the establishment of a caliphate in the manner of the Prophet and if we expect to establish its state predominantly-according to how it appears to us-in the heart of the Islamic world, then your efforts and sacrifices-God permitting-are a large step directly towards that goal.

So we must think for a long time about our next steps and how we want to attain it, and it is my humble opinion that the Jihad in Iraq requires several incremental goals:

The first stage: Expel the Americans from Iraq.

The second stage: Establish an Islamic authority or amirate, then develop it and support it until it achieves the level of a caliphate - over as much territory as you can to spread its power in Iraq, i.e., in Sunni areas, is in order to fill the void stemming from the departure of the Americans, immediately upon their exit and before un-Islamic forces attempt to fill this void, whether those whom the Americans will leave behind them, or those among the un-Islamic forces who will try to jump at taking power.

There is no doubt that this Emirate will enter into a fierce struggle with the foreign infidel forces, and those supporting them among the local forces, to put it in a state of constant preoccupation with defending itself, to make it impossible for it to establish a stable state which could proclaim a caliphate, and to keep the Jihadist groups in a constant state of war, until these forces find a chance to annihilate them.

The third stage: Extend the jihad wave to the secular countries neighboring Iraq.

The fourth stage: It may coincide with what came before: the clash with Israel, because Israel was established only to challenge any new Islamic entity.

My raising this idea - I don't claim that it's infallible - is only to stress something extremely important. And it is that the mujahideen must not have their mission end with the expulsion of the Americans from Iraq, and then lay down their weapons, and silence the fighting zeal. We will return to having the secularists and traitors holding sway over us. Instead, their ongoing mission is to establish an Islamic state, and defend it, and for every generation to hand over the banner to the one after it until the Hour of Resurrection.

If the matter is thus, we must contemplate our affairs carefully, so that we are not robbed of the spoils, and our brothers did not die, so that others can reap the fruits of their labor.

D.     If we look at the two short-term goals, which are removing the Americans and establishing an Islamic amirate in Iraq, or a caliphate if possible, then, we will see that the strongest weapon which the mujahedeen enjoy - after the help and granting of success by God - is popular support from the Muslim masses in Iraq, and the surrounding Muslim countries.

So, we must maintain this support as best we can, and we should strive to increase it, on the condition that striving for that support does not lead to any concession in the laws of the Sharia.

And it's very important that you allow me to elaborate a little here on this issue of popular support. Let's say:

(1) If we are in agreement that the victory of Islam and the establishment of a caliphate in the manner of  the Prophet will not be achieved except through jihad against the

apostate rulers and their removal, then this goal will not be accomplished by the mujahed movement while it is cut off from public support, even if the Jihadist movement pursues the method of sudden overthrow. This is because such an overthrow would not take place without some minimum of popular support and some condition of public discontent which offers the mujahed movement what it needs in terms of capabilities in the quickest fashion. Additionally, if the Jihadist movement were obliged to pursue other methods, such as a popular war of jihad or a popular intifadah, then popular support would be a decisive factor between victory and defeat.

(2) In the absence of this popular support, the Islamic mujahed movement would be crushed in the shadows, far from the masses who are distracted or fearful, and the struggle between the Jihadist elite and the arrogant authorities would be confined to prison dungeons far from the public and the light of day. This is precisely what the secular, apostate forces that are controlling our countries are striving for. These forces don't desire to wipe out the mujahed Islamic movement, rather they are stealthily striving to separate it from the misguided or frightened Muslim masses.

Therefore, our planning must strive to involve the Muslim masses in the battle, and to bring the mujahed movement to the masses and not conduct the struggle far from them.

(3) The Muslim masses-for many reasons, and this is not the place to discuss it-do not rally except against an outside occupying enemy, especially if the enemy is firstly Jewish, and secondly American.

This, in my limited opinion, is the reason for the popular support that the mujahedeen enjoy in Iraq, by the grace of God. As for the sectarian and chauvinistic factor, it is secondary in importance to outside aggression, and is much weaker than it. In my opinion-which is limited and which is what I see far from the scene-the awakening of the Sunni people in Iraq against the Shia would not have had such strength and toughness were it not for the treason of the Shia and their collusion with the Americans, and their agreement with them to permit the Americans to occupy Iraq in exchange for the Shia assuming power.

(4) Therefore, the mujahed movement must avoid any action that the masses do not understand or approve, if there is no contravention of Sharia in such avoidance, and as long as there are other options to resort to, meaning we must not throw the masses - scant in knowledge - into the sea before we teach them to swim, relying for guidance in that on

the saying of the Prophet to Umar bin al-Khattab: lest the people should say that Muhammad used to kill his Companions.

Among the practical applications of this viewpoint in your blessed arena:

## (A) The matter of preparing for the aftermath of the exit of the Americans:

The Americans will exit soon, God willing, and the establishment of a governing authority - as soon as the country is freed from the Americans-does not depend on force alone. Indeed, it's imperative that, in addition to force, there be an appeasement of Muslims and a sharing with them in governance and in the Shura council and in promulgating what is allowed and what is not allowed. In my view-which I continue to reiterate is limited and has a distant perspective upon the events-this must be achieved through the people of the Shura and who possess authority to determine issues and make them binding, and who are endowed with the qualifications for working in Sharia law. They would be elected by the people of the country to represent them and overlook the work of the authorities in accordance with the rules of the glorious Sharia.

And it doesn't appear that the Mujahedeen, much less the al-Qaida in the Land of Two Rivers, will lay claim to governance without the Iraqi people. Not to mention that that would be in contravention of the Shura methodology. That is not practical in my opinion.

You might ask an important question: What drives me to broach these matters while we are in the din of war and the challenges of killing and combat?

My answer is, firstly: Things may develop faster than we imagine. The aftermath of the collapse of American power in Vietnam - and how they ran and left their agents - is noteworthy. Because of that, we must be ready starting now, before events overtake us, and before we are surprised by the conspiracies of the Americans and the United Nations and their plans to fill the void behind them. We must take the initiative and impose a fait accompli upon our enemies, instead of the enemy imposing one on us, wherein our lot would be to merely resist their schemes.

Second: This is the most vital part. This authority, or the Sharia amirate that is necessary, requires fieldwork starting now, alongside the combat and war. It would be a political endeavor in which the mujahedeen would be a nucleus around which would gather the tribes and their elders, and the people in positions, and scientists, and merchants, and people of opinion, and all the distinguished ones who were not sullied by appeasing the occupation and those who defended Islam.

We don't want to repeat the mistake of the Taliban, who restricted participation in governance to the students and the people of Qandahar alone. They did not have any representation for the Afghan people in their ruling regime, so the result was that the Afghan people disengaged themselves from them. Even devout ones took the stance of the spectator and, when the invasion came, the amirate collapsed in days, because the people were either passive or hostile. Even the students themselves had a stronger affiliation to their tribes and their villages than their affiliation to the Islamic amirate or the Taliban movement or the responsible party in charge of each one of them in his place.

Each of them retreated to his village and his tribe, where his affiliation was stronger!!

The comparison between the fall of Kabul and the resistance of Fallujah, Ramadi, and Al Qaim and their fearless sisters shows a clear distinction, by God's grace and His kindness. It is the matter towards which we must strive, that we must support and strengthen.

Therefore, I stress again to you and to all your brothers the need to direct the political action equally with the military action, by the alliance, cooperation and gathering of all leaders of opinion and influence in the Iraqi arena. I can't define for you a specific means of action. You are more knowledgeable about the field conditions. But you and your brothers must strive to have around you circles of support, assistance, and cooperation, and through them, to advance until you become a consensus, entity, organization, or association that represents all the honorable people and the loyal folks in Iraq. I repeat the warning against separating from the masses, whatever the danger.

**(2) Striving for the unity of the mujahedeen:**

This is something I entrust to you. It is between you and God. If the mujahedeen are scattered, this leads to the scattering of the people around them. I don't have detailed information about the situation of the mujahedeen, so I ask that you help us with some beneficial details in this, and the extent of the different mujahedeen movements' readiness to join the course of unity.

**(3) Striving for the ulema:**

From the standpoint of not highlighting the doctrinal differences which the masses do not understand, such as this one is Matridi or this one is Ashari or this one is Salafi, and from the standpoint of doing justice to the people, for there may be in the world a heresy or an inadequacy in a side which may have something to give to jihad, fighting, and sacrifice for God.

We have seen magnificent examples in the Afghan jihad, and the prince of believers, Mullah Muhammad Omar - may God protect him - himself is of Hanafi adherence, Matridi doctrine, but he stood in the history of Islam with a stance rarely taken. You are the richer if you know the stances of the authentic ulema on rulers in times of jihad and the defense of the Muslim holy sites. And more than that, their stances on doing justice to the people and not denying their merit.

The ulema among the general public are, as well, the symbol of Islam and its emblem.

Their disparagement may lead to the general public deeming religion and its adherents as being unimportant. This is a greater injury than the benefit of criticizing a theologian on a heresy or an issue.

Of course, these words of mine have nothing to do with the hypocritical traitors who are

in allegiance with the crusaders, but I wish to stress the warning against diminishing the ulema before the general public.

Also, the active mujahedeen ulema - even if there may be some heresy or fault in them that is not blasphemous - we must find a means to include them and to benefit from their energy. You know well -what I am mentioning to you- that many of the most learned ulema of Islam such as Izz Bin Abdul Salam, al-Nawawi, and Ibn Hajar - may God have mercy on them - were Ashari. And many of the most eminent jihadists, whom the Umma resolved unanimously to praise such as Nur al-Din Bin Zanki and Salah-al-Din al-Ayyubi - were Ashari.

The mujahedeen sultans who came after them - who didn't reach their level - whom the ulema and the historians lauded such as Sayf al-Din Qatz, Rukn al-Din Baybars, al-Nasir Muhammad Bin-Qallawun, and Muhammad al-Fatih, were Ashari or Matridi. They fell into errors, sins, and heresies. And the stances of Sheikh al-Islam Ibn Taymiya regarding al-Nasir Muhammad Bin Qallawun and his extolling of him and his inciting him to jihad - despite the prosecutions and prison which befell the sheikh in his time - are well known.

If you take into account the fact that most of the Umma's ulema are Ashari or Matridi,

and if you take into consideration as well the fact that the issue of correcting the mistakes of ideology is an issue that will require generations of the call to Islam and modifying the educational curricula, and that the mujahedeen are not able to undertake this burden, rather they are in need of those who will help them with the difficulties and problems they face; if you take all this into consideration, and add to it the fact that all Muslims are speaking of jihad, whether they are Salafi or non-Salafi, then you would understand that it is a duty of the mujahed movement to include the energies of the Umma and in its wisdom and prudence to fill the role of leader, trailblazer, and exploiter of all the capabilities of the Umma for the sake of achieving our aims: a caliphate along the lines of the Prophet's, with God's permission.

I do not know the details of the situation where you are, but I do not want us to repeat the mistake of Jamil al-Rahman~, who was killed and whose organization was shattered, because he neglected the realities on the ground.

**(4) The position on the Shia:**

This subject is complicated and detailed. I have brought it up here so as not to address the general public on something they do not know. But please permit me to present it logically:

(A) I repeat that I see the picture from afar, and I repeat that you see what we do not see. No doubt you have the right to defend yourself, the mujahedeen, and Muslims in general and in particular against any aggression or threat of aggression.

(B) I assert here that any rational person understands with ease that the Shia cooperated with the Americans in the invasion of Afghanistan, Rafsanjani himself confessed to it, and they cooperated with them in the overthrow of Saddam and the occupation of Iraq in exchange for the Shia's assumption of power and their turning a blind eye to the American military presence in Iraq. This is clear to everybody who has two eyes.

(C) People of discernment and knowledge among Muslims know the extent of danger to Islam of the Twelve'er school of Shiism. It is a religious school based on excess and falsehood whose function is to accuse the companions of Muhammad of heresy in a campaign against Islam, in order to free the way for a group of those who call for a dialogue in the name of the hidden mahdi who is in control of existence and infallible in what he does. Their prior history in cooperating with the enemies of Islam is consistent with their current reality of connivance with the Crusaders.

(D) The collision between any state based on the model of prophecy with the Shia is a matter that will happen sooner or later. This is the judgment of history, and these are the fruits to be expected from the rejectionist Shia sect and their opinion of the Sunnis.

These are clear, well-known matters to anyone with a knowledge of history, the ideologies, and the politics of states.

(E) We must repeat what we mentioned previously, that the majority of Muslims don't comprehend this and possibly could not even imagine it. For that reason, many of your Muslim admirers amongst the common folk are wondering about your attacks on the Shia. The sharpness of this questioning increases when the attacks are on one of their mosques, and it increases more when the attacks are on the mausoleum of Imam Ali Bin Abi Talib, may God honor him. My opinion is that this matter won't be acceptable to the Muslim populace however much you have tried to explain it, and aversion to this will continue.

Indeed, questions will circulate among mujahedeen circles and their opinion makers about the correctness of this conflict with the Shia at this time. Is it something that is unavoidable? Or, is it something can be put off until the force of the mujahed movement in Iraq gets stronger? And if some of the operations were necessary for self-defense, were all of the operations necessary? Or, were there some operations that weren't called for?

And is the opening of another front now in addition to the front against the Americans and the government a wise decision? Or, does this conflict with the Shia lift the burden from the Americans by diverting the mujahedeen to the Shia, while the Americans continue to control matters from afar? And if the attacks on Shia leaders were necessary to put a stop to their plans, then why were there attacks on ordinary Shia?

Won't this lead to reinforcing  false ideas in their minds, even as it is incumbent on us to preach the call of Islam to them and explain and communicate to guide them to the truth? And can the mujahedeen kill all of the Shia in Iraq? Has any Islamic state in history ever tried that? And why kill ordinary Shia considering that they are forgiven because of their ignorance? And what loss will befall us if we did not attack the Shia?

And do the brothers forget that we have more than one hundred prisoners  - many of whom are from the leadership who are wanted in their countries - in the custody of the Iranians? And even if we attack the Shia out of necessity, then why do you announce this matter and make it public, which compels the Iranians to take counter measures? And do the brothers forget that both we and the Iranians need to refrain from harming each other at this time in which the Americans are targeting us?

All of these questions and others are circulating among your brothers, and they are monitoring the picture from afar, as I told you. One who monitors from afar lacks many of the important details that affect decision-making in the field.

However, monitoring from afar has the advantage of providing the total picture and observing the general line without getting submerged in the details, which might draw attention away from the direction of the target. As the English proverb says, the person who is standing among the leaves of the tree might not see the tree.

One of the most important factors of success is that you don't let your eyes lose sight of the target, and that it should stand before you always. Otherwise you deviate from the general line through a policy of reaction. And this is a lifetime's experience, and I will not conceal from you the fact that we suffered a lot through following this policy of reaction, then we suffered a lot another time because we tried to return to the original line.

One of the most important things facing the leadership is the enthusiasm of the supporters, and especially of the energetic young men who are burning to make the religion victorious. This enthusiasm must flow wisely, and al-Mutanabbi says:

Courage in a man does suffice but not like the courage of one who is wise.

And he also says:

Judiciousness precedes the courage of the courageous which is second  And when the two blend in one free soul it reaches everywhere in the heavens.

In summation, with regard to the talk about the issue of the Shia, I would like to repeat that I see that matter from afar without being aware of all the details, I would like my words to be deserving of your attention and consideration, and God is the  guarantor of success for every good thing.

(5) Scenes of slaughter:

Among the things which the feelings of the Muslim populace who love and support you will never find palatable  - also- are the scenes of slaughtering the hostages. You shouldn't be deceived by the praise of some of the zealous young men and their description of you as the shaykh of the slaughterers, etc. They do not express the general view of the admirer and the supporter of the resistance in Iraq, and of you in particular by the favor and blessing of God.

And your response, while true, might be: Why shouldn't we sow terror in the hearts of the Crusaders and their helpers? And isn't the destruction of the villages and the cities on the heads of their inhabitants more cruel than slaughtering? And aren't the cluster bombs and the seven ton bombs and the depleted uranium bombs crueler than  slaughtering? And isn't killing by torture crueler than slaughtering? And isn't violating the honor of men and women more painful and more destructive than slaughtering?

All of these questions and more might be asked, and you are justified. However this does not change the reality at all, which is that the general opinion of our supporter does not comprehend that, and that this general opinion falls under a campaign by the malicious, perfidious, and fallacious campaign by the deceptive and fabricated media.

And we would spare the people from the effect of questions about the usefulness of our actions in the hearts and minds of the general opinion that is essentially sympathetic to us.

And I say to you with sure feeling and I say: That the author of these lines has tasted  the bitterness of American brutality, and that my favorite wife's chest was crushed by a concrete ceiling and she went on calling for aid to lift the stone block off her chest until she breathed her last, may God have mercy on her and accept her among the martyrs.

As for my young daughter, she was afflicted by a cerebral hemorrhage, and she continued for a whole day suffering in pain until she expired. And to this day I do not know the location of the graves of my wife, my son, my daughter, and the rest of the three other families who were martyred in the incident and who were pulverized by the concrete ceiling, may God have mercy on them and the Muslim martyrs. Were they brought out of the rubble, or are they still buried beneath it to this day?

However, despite all of this, I say to you: that we are in a battle, and that more than half of this battle is taking place in the battlefield of the media. And that we are in a media battle in a race for the hearts and minds of our Umma. And that however far our capabilities reach, they will never be equal to one thousandth of the capabilities of the kingdom of Satan that is waging war on us. And we can kill the captives by bullet. That would achieve that which is sought after without exposing ourselves to the questions and answering to doubts. We don't need this.

E - I would like you to explain for us another issue related to Iraq, and I think without a doubt that you are the most knowledgeable about it. Can the assumption of leadership for the mujahedeen or a group of the mujahedeen by non-Iraqis stir up sensitivity for some people? And if there is sensitivity, what is its effect? And how can it be eliminated while preserving the commitment of the jihadist work and without exposing it to any shocks? Please inform us in detail regarding this matter.

F - Likewise I would like you to inform us about the Iraqi situation in general and the situation of the mujahedeen in particular in detail without exposing the security of the mujahedeen and the Muslims to danger. At the least, we should know as much as the enemy knows. And allow us to burden you with this trouble, for we are most eager to learn your news.

G - I have a definite desire to travel to you but I do not know whether that is possible from the standpoint of traveling and getting settled, so please let me know. And God is the guarantor of every good thing.

5 - Please take every caution in the meetings, especially when someone claims to carry an

important letter or contributions. It was in this way that they arrested Khalid Sheikh.

Likewise, please, if you want to meet one of your assistants, I hope that you don't meet him in a public place or in a place that is not known to you. I hope that you would meet him in a secure place, not the place of your residence. Because Abu al-Faraj - may God set him free and release him from his torment - was lured by one of his brothers, who had been taken into custody, to meet him at a public location where a trap had been set.

6 - The brothers informed me that you suggested to them sending some assistance. Our situation since Abu al-Faraj is good by the grace of God, but many of the lines have been cut off. Because of this, we need a payment while new lines are being opened. So, if you're capable of sending a payment of approximately one hundred thousand, we'll be very grateful to you.

7 - The subject of the Algerian brothers at our end, there are fears from the previous experiences, so if you're able to get in touch with them and notify us of the details from them, we would be very grateful to you.

8-As for news on the poor servant,

A-During an earlier period I published some publications:

(1) Allegiance and exemption - A Faith transmitted, a lost reality.

(2) Strengthening the Banner of Islam - an article emphasizing the authority's commitment to monotheism.

(3) Wind of Paradise - an article about: Most Honorable Sacrifices of the Believers - Campaigns of Death and Martyrdom. I endeavored in this article to include what was written on the subject as much as I could. I also strived to verify every word in it, and it's an issue that took me almost a year or more.

(4) The Bitter Harvest - The Muslim Brotherhood in 60 Years - Second Edition 1426h - 2005m.

In this edition, I wanted to delete all the extreme phrases for which there's no proof, and I referred to the book a number of times, then I wrote a new preface. In it I pointed out a dangerous trend of the Brotherhood, especially in the circumstances of the New Crusader War which was launched on the Islamic Umma. In my opinion, this edition is better than the first with respect to the calmness of the presentation instead of being emotional. The Brotherhood's danger is demonstrated by the weakening of the Islamic Resistance to the campaign of the Crusaders and their supporters. God is the only one who is perfect.

(5) I have also had fifteen audio statements published and six others that were not published for one reason or another. We ask God for acceptance and devotion.

I will enclose for you the written statements and what I can of the audio and video statements with this message, God willing. If you find they are good, you can publish them. We seek God's assistance.

(6) I don't know if you all have contact with Abu Rasmi? Even if it is via the Internet, because I gave him a copy of my book (Knights Under the Prophets Banner) so he could attempt to publish it, and I lost the original. Al-Sharq al-Awsat newspaper published it truncated and jumbled. I think that the American intelligence services provided the aforementioned newspaper with it from my computer which they acquired, because the publication of the book coincided with a publication of messages from my computer in the same newspaper. So if you can contact him and get the original of the book, if that is possible for you all, then you can publish it on your blessed website and then send a copy to us, if that is possible.

B - As for my personal condition, I am in good health, blessings and wellness thanks to God and His grace. I am only lacking your pious prayers, in which I beg you not to forget me. God Almighty has blessed me with a daughter whom I have named (Nawwar), and Nawwar means: the timid female gazelle and the woman who is free from suspicion, and technically: it is the name of my maternal aunt who was a second mother to me and who stood with me during all the difficult and harsh times. I ask God to reward her for me with the best reward, and have mercy on her, our mothers and the Muslims.

9 - My greetings to all the loved ones and please give me news of Karem and the rest of the folks I know, and especially:

By God, if by chance you're going to Fallujah, send greetings to Abu Musab al-Zarqawi.

In closing, I ask God entrust you all with His guardianship, providence and protection, and bless you all in your families, possessions and offspring and protect them from all evil and that He delight you all with them in this world and the next world, and that He bestow upon us and you all the victory that he promised his servants the Believers, and that He strengthen for us our religion which He has sanctioned for us, and that He make us safe after our fear.Peace, God's blessings and mercy to you.

Your loving brother

Abu Muhammad

Saturday, 02 Jumada al-Thani, 1426 - 09 July, 2005.

## Message to the British
## Dr. Ayman Zawahiri
## August 4, 2005

And to the English, to all of them: the lies and the actions of Blair are responsible for bringing destruction to you, to the center of London, and he will bring you more of the same, inshahallah (Allah willing).

To them, and to the other unbelievers (kuffar) in the coalition (alliance) of the Crusaders, we have offered you, at least, to stop your aggression against the Muslims.

We have offered you.

The lion of Islam, the mujahid Sheik Osama bin Laden, may Allah protect him, before offered you a truce, if you would leave the lands of Islam.

Did they not learn when Sheik Osama bin Laden told you that you could not dream of security before these things are done: before we live in peace and security as a reality in Palestine, and before all of the armies of the Kuffars leave the lands of Mohamed, peace be upon?

But instead you have created rivers of blood in our countries, so we blew up volcanoes of rage in your countries.

Our message to you is clear, nonnegotiable, and you must do it immediately: There will be no saving you except if you meet these three conditions: You must withdraw from all our lands. You must stop stealing out petroleum and our other riches. And you must immediately stop supporting the corrupt leaders.

<tape appears to be spliced here>

The things, you Americans, that you have seen in New York and Washington, and the losses you witness in Afghanistan and in Iraq, in spite of all the media hiding it, are nothing but the casualties of the beginning battles. But if you keep following the same policy of aggression against the Muslim people, you will see, God willing, more horrors that will make you forget all that you saw in Afghanistan... umm umm, in Vietnam.

<tape appears to be spliced here>

The truth that Bush, Rice and Rumsfeld hide from you is that there is no way to escape Iraq, except by withdrawing immediately, and that any delay in making this decision means nothing but more dead and more wounded. .

But if you don't leave today, you will most certainly leave tomorrow, but you will leave after tens of thousands die, and many more are crippled and wounded.

And all of the same lies they said about Vietnam, they repeat today about Iraq. Did they not say that they would train the Vietnamese to manage their own affairs, and that they were there defending freedom in Vietnam?

## October 22, 2005
## Dr. Ayman al-Zawahiri

*Translator's Note: This is the message released by Zawahiri in response to the earthquake in Pakistan. In the tape, he calls upon Muslims to send aid to their Muslim brothers in the affected areas.*

We have sadly received the news of the disaster that befell the Pakistani Muslim people following the earthquake that struck the region.

We ask Allah (God) to grant those killed in the earthquake the positions of martyrs and pious people.

My brothers and myself wish to be among you, our dear brothers, on this day.

However, agents of America are standing in our way to help our Muslim brothers in their distress.

Today, I call on Muslims in general, and on Islamic relief organisations in particular, to go to Pakistan and help their Pakistani brothers and withstand the troubles and harm they face for this purpose.

We all know the raging American war against Islamic charitable work.

We all know that Musharraf's government is a chip of the American intelligence.

However, despite all this, I urge all Muslims to rush in helping their brothers in Pakistan by all means and by transferring as much aid as possible,

## January 6, 2006
## Ayman al-Zawahiri
## Condolences to Pakistan on the Earthquake

*Translator's Note:* *This video was released by Sahab Media on the internet, and includes English subtitles.*

Even though I send my condolences to my Islamic nation for the tragedy of the earthquake in Pakistan, today I congratulate everyone for the victory in Iraq. You remember, my dear Muslim brethren, what I told you more than a year ago, that the U.S. troops will pull out of Iraq. It was only a matter of time.

Here they are now and in the blessing of God begging to pull out, seeking negotiations with the mujahedeen. And here is Bush who was forced to announce at the end of last November that he will be pulling his troops out of Iraq.

He uses the pretext that the Iraqi forces reached a high level of preparedness. But he doesn't have a timetable for the pullout.

If all of his troops -- air force, army -- are begging for a way to get out of Iraq, will the liars, traitors and infidels succeed in what the world superpower failed to achieve in Iraq?

You have set the timetable for the withdrawal a long time ago and Bush, you have to admit that you were defeated in Iraq, you are being defeated in Afghanistan, and you will be defeated in Palestine, God willing.

## Letter to the Americans:
## Why do we fight and resist you?
## Dr. Ayman al-Zawahiri
## January 10, 2006

*Translator's Note:  This video was released by Sahab Media and shows a photograph of Zawahiri, with English text on the screen.  An English-language audio plays in the background.  Although this is not per se a Zawahiri video, I am including it because his image is used with the voice-over.*

*The text of the video is an English translation of a letter to the United States penned by Osama Bin Laden in November 2002.*

In the Name of Allah, the Most Gracious, the Most Merciful,

"Permission to fight (against disbelievers) is given to those (believers) who are fought against, because they have been wronged and surely, Allah is Able to give them (believers) victory" [Quran 22:39]

"Those who believe, fight in the Cause of Allah, and those who disbelieve, fight in the cause of Taghut (anything worshipped other than Allah e.g. Satan). So fight you against the friends of Satan; ever feeble is indeed the plot of Satan."[Quran 4:76]

By Laura Mansfield

Some American writers have published articles under the title 'On what basis are we fighting?' These articles have generated a number of responses, some of which adhered to the truth and were based on Islamic Law, and others which have not. Here we wanted to outline the truth - as an explanation and warning - hoping for Allah's reward, seeking success and support from Him.

While seeking Allah's help, we form our reply based on two questions directed at the Americans:

(Q1) Why are we fighting and opposing you?

Q2)What are we calling you to, and what do we want from you?

As for the first question: Why are we fighting and opposing you? The answer is very simple:

(1) Because you attacked us and continue to attack us.

a) You attacked us in Palestine:

(i) Palestine, which has sunk under military occupation for more than 80 years. The British handed over Palestine, with your help and your support, to the Jews, who have occupied it for more than 50 years; years overflowing with oppression, tyranny, crimes, killing, expulsion, destruction and devastation. The

288

creation and continuation of Israel is one of the greatest crimes, and you are the leaders of its criminals. And of course there is no need to explain and prove the degree of American support for Israel. The creation of Israel is a crime which must be erased. Each and every person whose hands have become polluted in the contribution towards this crime must pay its*price, and pay for it heavily.

(ii) It brings us both laughter and tears to see that you have not yet tired of repeating your fabricated lies that the Jews have a historical right to Palestine, as it was promised to them in the Torah. Anyone who disputes with them on this alleged fact is accused of anti-semitism. This is one of the most fallacious, widely-circulated fabrications in history. The people of Palestine are pure Arabs and original Semites. It is the Muslims who are the inheritors of Moses (peace be upon him) and the inheritors of the real Torah that has not been changed. Muslims believe in all of the Prophets, including Abraham, Moses, Jesus and Muhammad, peace and blessings of Allah be upon them all. If the followers of Moses have been promised a right to Palestine in the Torah, then the Muslims are the most worthy nation of this.

When the Muslims conquered Palestine and drove out the Romans, Palestine and Jerusalem returned to Islaam, the religion of all the Prophets peace be upon them. Therefore, the call to a historical right to Palestine cannot be raised against the Islamic Ummah that believes in all the Prophets of Allah (peace and blessings be upon them) - and we make no distinction between them.

(iii) The blood pouring out of Palestine must be equally revenged. You must know that the Palestinians do not cry alone; their women are not widowed alone; their sons are not orphaned alone.

(b) You attacked us in Somalia; you supported the Russian atrocities against us in Chechnya, the Indian oppression against us in Kashmir, and the Jewish aggression against us in Lebanon.

(c) Under your supervision, consent and orders, the governments of our countries which act as your agents, attack us on a daily basis;

(i) These governments prevent our people from establishing the Islamic Shariah, using violence and lies to do so.

(ii) These governments give us a taste of humiliation, and places us in a large prison of fear and subdual.

(iii) These governments steal our Ummah's wealth and sell them to you at a paltry price.

(iv) These governments have surrendered to the Jews, and handed them most of Palestine, acknowledging the existence of their state over the dismembered limbs of their own people.

(v) The removal of these governments is an obligation upon us, and a necessary step to free the Ummah, to make the Shariah the supreme law and to regain Palestine. And our fight against these governments is not separate from out fight against you.

(d) You steal our wealth and oil at paltry prices because of you international influence and military threats. This theft is indeed the biggest theft ever witnessed by mankind in the history of the world.

(e) Your forces occupy our countries; you spread your military bases throughout them; you corrupt our lands, and you besiege our sanctities, to protect the security of the Jews and to ensure the continuity of your pillage of our treasures.

(f) You have starved the Muslims of Iraq, where children die every day. It is a wonder that more than 1.5 million Iraqi children have died as a result of your sanctions, and you did not show concern. Yet when 3000 of your people died, the entire world rises and has not yet sat down.

(g) You have supported the Jews in their idea that Jerusalem is their eternal capital, and agreed to move your embassy there. With your help and under your protection, the Israelis are planning to destroy the Al-Aqsa mosque. Under the protection of your weapons, Sharon entered the Al-Aqsa mosque, to pollute it as a preparation to capture and destroy it.

(2) These tragedies and calamities are only a few examples of your oppression and aggression against us. It is commanded by our religion and intellect that the oppressed have a right to return the aggression. Do not await anything from us but Jihad, resistance and revenge. Is it in any way rational to expect that after America has attacked us for more than half a century, that we will then leave her to live in security and peace?!!

(3) You may then dispute that all the above does not justify aggression against civilians, for crimes they did not commit and offenses in which they did not partake:

(a) This argument contradicts your continuous repetition that America is the land of freedom, and its leaders in this world. Therefore, the American people are the ones who choose their government by way of their own free will; a choice which stems from their agreement to its policies. Thus the American people have chosen, consented to, and affirmed their support for the Israeli oppression of the Palestinians, the occupation and usurpation of their land, and its continuous killing, torture, punishment and expulsion of the Palestinians. The American people have the ability and choice to refuse the policies of their Government and even to change it if they want.

(b) The American people are the ones who pay the taxes which fund the planes that bomb us in Afghanistan, the tanks that strike and destroy our homes in Palestine, the armies which occupy our lands in the Arabian Gulf, and the fleets which ensure the blockade of Iraq. These tax dollars are given to Israel for it to continue to attack us and penetrate our lands. So the American people are the ones who fund the attacks against us, and they are the ones who oversee the expenditure of these monies in the way they wish, through their elected candidates.

(c) Also the American army is part of the American people. It is this very same people who are shamelessly helping the Jews fight against us.

(d) The American people are the ones who employ both their men and their women in the American Forces which attack us.

(e) This is why the American people cannot be not innocent of all the crimes committed by the Americans and Jews against us.

(f) Allah, the Almighty, legislated the permission and the option to take revenge. Thus, if we are attacked, then we have the right to attack back. Whoever has destroyed our villages and towns, then we have the right to destroy their villages and towns. Whoever has stolen our wealth, then we have the right to destroy their economy. And whoever has killed our civilians, then we have the right to kill theirs.

The American Government and press still refuses to answer the question:

Why did they attack us in New York and Washington?

If Sharon is a man of peace in the eyes of Bush, then we are also men of peace!!! America does not understand the language of manners and principles, so we are addressing it using the language it understands.

(Q2) As for the second question that we want to answer: What are we calling you to, and what do we want from you?

(1) The first thing that we are calling you to is Islam.

(a) The religion of the Unification of God; of freedom from associating partners with Him, and rejection of this; of complete love of Him, the Exalted; of complete submission to His Laws; and of the discarding of all the opinions, orders, theories and religions which contradict with the religion He sent down to His Prophet Muhammad (peace be upon him). Islam is the religion of all the prophets, and makes no distinction between them - peace be upon them all.

It is to this religion that we call you; the seal of all the previous religions. It is the religion of Unification of God, sincerity, the best of manners, righteousness, mercy, honour, purity, and piety. It is the religion of showing kindness to others, establishing justice between them, granting them their rights, and defending the oppressed and the persecuted. It is the religion of enjoining the good and forbidding the evil with the hand, tongue and heart. It is the religion of Jihad in the way of Allah so that Allah's Word and religion reign Supreme. And it is the religion of unity and agreement on the obedience to Allah, and total equality between all people, without regarding their colour, sex, or language.

(b) It is the religion whose book - the Quran - will remained preserved and unchanged, after the other Divine books and messages have been changed. The Quran is the miracle until the Day of Judgment. Allah has challenged anyone to bring a book like the Quran or even ten verses like it.

(2) The second thing we call you to, is to stop your oppression, lies, immorality and debauchery that has spread among you.

(a) We call you to be a people of manners, principles, honour, and purity; to reject the immoral acts of fornication, homosexuality, intoxicants, gambling's, and trading with interest.

We call you to all of this that you may be freed from that which you have become caught up in; that you may be freed from the deceptive lies that you are a great nation, that your leaders spread amongst you to conceal from you the despicable state to which you have reached.

(b) It is saddening to tell you that you are the worst civilization witnessed by the history of mankind:

(i) You are the nation who, rather than ruling by the Shariah of Allah in its Constitution and Laws, choose to invent your own laws as you will and desire. You separate religion from

296

your policies, contradicting the pure nature which affirms Absolute Authority to the Lord and your Creator. You flee from the embarrassing question posed to you: How is it possible for Allah the Almighty to create His creation, grant them power over all the creatures and land, grant them all the amenities of life, and then deny them that which they are most in need of: knowledge of the laws which govern their lives?

(ii) You are the nation that permits Usury, which has been forbidden by all the religions. Yet you build your economy and investments on Usury. As a result of this, in all its different forms and guises, the Jews have taken control of your economy, through which they have then taken control of your media, and now control all aspects of your life making you their servants and achieving their aims at your expense; precisely what Benjamin Franklin warned you against.

(iii) You are a nation that permits the production, trading and usage of intoxicants. You also permit drugs, and only forbid the trade of them, even though your nation is the largest consumer of them.

(iv) You are a nation that permits acts of immorality, and you consider them to be pillars of personal freedom. You have continued to sink down this abyss from level to level until incest has spread amongst you, in the face of which neither your sense of honour nor your laws object.

Who can forget your President Clinton's immoral acts committed in the official Oval office? After that you did not even bring him to account, other than that he 'made a mistake', after which everything passed with no punishment. Is there a worse kind of event for which your name will go down in history and remembered by nations?

(v) You are a nation that permits gambling in its all forms. The companies practice this as well, resulting in the investments becoming active and the criminals becoming rich.

(vi) You are a nation that exploits women like consumer products or advertising tools calling upon customers to purchase them. You use women to serve passengers, visitors, and strangers to increase your profit margins. You then rant that you support the liberation of women.

(vii) You are a nation that practices the trade of sex in all its forms, directly and indirectly. Giant corporations and establishments are established on this, under the name of art, entertainment, tourism and freedom, and other deceptive names you attribute to it.

(viii) And because of all this, you have been described in history as a nation that spreads diseases that were unknown to man in the past. Go ahead and boast to the nations of man, that you brought them AIDS as a Satanic American Invention.

(xi) You have destroyed nature with your industrial waste and gases more than any other nation in history. Despite this, you refuse to sign the Kyoto agreement so that you can secure the profit of your greedy companies and*industries.

(x) Your law is the law of the rich and wealthy people, who hold sway in their political parties, and fund their election campaigns with their gifts. Behind them stand the Jews, who control your policies, media and economy.

(xi) That which you are singled out for in the history of mankind, is that you have used your force to destroy mankind more than any other nation in history; not to defend principles and values, but to hasten to secure your interests and profits. You who dropped a nuclear bomb on Japan, even though Japan was ready to negotiate an end to the war. How many acts of oppression, tyranny and injustice have you carried out, O callers to freedom?

(xii) Let us not forget one of your major characteristics: your duality in both manners and values; your hypocrisy in manners and principles. All*manners, principles and values have two scales: one for you and one for the others.

(a)The freedom and democracy that you call to is for yourselves and for white race only; as for the rest of the world, you impose upon them your monstrous, destructive policies and Governments, which you call the 'American friends'. Yet you prevent them from establishing democracies. When the Islamic party in Algeria wanted to practice democracy and they won the election, you unleashed your agents in the Algerian army onto them, and to attack them with tanks and guns, to imprison them and torture them - a new lesson from the 'American book of democracy'!!!

(b)Your policy on prohibiting and forcibly removing weapons of mass destruction to ensure world peace: it only applies to those countries which you do not permit to possess such weapons. As for the countries you consent to, such as Israel, then they are allowed to keep and use such weapons to defend their security. Anyone else who you suspect might be manufacturing or keeping these kinds of weapons, you call them criminals and you take military action against them.

(c)You are the last ones to respect the resolutions and policies of International Law, yet you claim to want to selectively punish anyone else who does the same. Israel has for more than 50 years been pushing UN resolutions and rules against the wall with the full support of America.

(d)As for the war criminals which you censure and form criminal courts for - you shamelessly ask that your own are granted immunity!! However, history will not forget the war crimes that you committed against the Muslims and the rest of the world; those you have killed in Japan, Afghanistan, Somalia, Lebanon and Iraq will remain a shame that you will never be able to escape. It will suffice to remind you of your latest war crimes in Afghanistan, in which densely populated innocent civilian villages were destroyed, bombs were dropped on mosques causing the roof of the mosque to come crashing down on the heads of the Muslims praying inside. You are the ones who broke the agreement with the Mujahideen when they left Qunduz, bombing them in Jangi fort, and killing more than 1,000 of your prisoners through suffocation and thirst. Allah alone knows how many people have died by torture at the hands of you and your agents. Your planes remain in the Afghan skies, looking for anyone remotely suspicious.

(e)You have claimed to be the vanguards of Human Rights, and your Ministry of Foreign affairs issues annual reports containing statistics of those countries that violate any Human Rights. However, all these things vanished when the Mujahideen hit you, and you then implemented the methods of the same documented governments that you used to curse. In America, you captured thousands the Muslims and Arabs, took them into custody with neither reason, court trial, nor even disclosing their names. You issued newer, harsher laws.

What happens in Guatanamo is a historical embarrassment to America and its values, and it screams into your faces - you hypocrites, "What is the value of your signature on any agreement or treaty?"

(3) What we call you to thirdly is to take an honest stance with yourselves - and I doubt you will do so - to discover that you are a nation without principles or manners, and that the values and principles to you are something which you merely demand from others, not that which you yourself must adhere to.

(4) We also advise you to stop supporting Israel, and to end your support of the Indians in Kashmir, the Russians against the Chechens and to also cease supporting the Manila

Government against the Muslims in Southern Philippines.

(5) We also advise you to pack your luggage and get out of our lands. We desire for your goodness, guidance, and righteousness, so do not force us to send you back as cargo in coffins.

(6) Sixthly, we call upon you to end your support of the corrupt leaders in our countries. Do not interfere in our politics and method of education. Leave us alone, or else expect us in New York and Washington.

(7) We also call you to deal with us and interact with us on the basis of mutual interests and benefits, rather than the policies of sub dual, theft and occupation, and not to continue your policy of supporting the Jews because this will result in more disasters for you.

If you fail to respond to all these conditions, then prepare for fight with the Islamic Nation. The Nation of Monotheism, that puts complete trust on Allah and fears none other than Him. The Nation which is addressed by its Quran with the words: "Do you fear them? Allah has more right that you should fear Him if you are believers. Fight against them so that Allah will punish them by your hands and disgrace them and give you victory over them and heal the breasts of believing people. And remove the anger of their (believers') hearts. Allah accepts the repentance of whom He wills. Allah is All-Knowing, All-Wise." [Quran9:13-1]

The Nation of honour and respect:

"But honour, power and glory belong to Allah, and to His Messenger (Muhammad- peace be upon him) and to the believers." [Quran 63:8]

"So do not become weak (against your enemy), nor be sad, and you will be*superior ( in victory )if you are indeed (true) believers" [Quran 3:139]

The Nation of Martyrdom; the Nation that desires death more than you desire life:

"Think not of those who are killed in the way of Allah as dead. Nay, they are alive with their Lord, and they are being provided for. They rejoice in what Allah has bestowed upon them from His bounty and rejoice for the sake of those who have not yet joined them, but are left behind (not yet martyred) that on them no fear shall come, nor shall they grieve. They rejoice in a grace and a bounty from Allah, and that Allah will not waste the reward of the believers." [Quran 3:169-171]

The Nation of victory and success that Allah has promised:

"It is He Who has sent His Messenger (Muhammad peace be upon him) with guidance and the religion of truth (Islam), to make it victorious over all other religions even though the Polytheists hate it." [Quran 61:9]

"Allah has decreed that 'Verily it is I and My Messengers who shall be victorious.' Verily Allah is All-Powerful, All-Mighty." [Quran 58:21]

The Islamic Nation that was able to dismiss and destroy the previous evil Empires like yourself; the Nation that rejects your attacks, wishes to remove your evils, and is prepared to fight you. You are well aware that the Islamic Nation, from the very core of its soul, despises your haughtiness and arrogance.

If the Americans refuse to listen to our advice and the goodness, guidance and righteousness that we call them to, then be aware that you will lose this Crusade Bush began, just like the other previous Crusades in which you were humiliated by the hands of the Mujahideen, fleeing to your home in great silence and disgrace. If the Americans do not respond, then their fate will be that of the Soviets who fled from Afghanistan to deal with their military defeat, political breakup, ideological downfall, and economic bankruptcy.

This is our message to the Americans, as an answer to theirs. Do they now know why we fight them and over which form of ignorance, by the permission of Allah, we shall be victorious?

## January 30, 2006
## Dr. Ayman al-Zawahiri

*Translator's note:* *This video was released shortly after reports emerged speculating about Zawahiri's death in an American air strike in Pakistan. The video release put to bed rumors of Zawahiri's death. Many refer to this video as his "I'm Alive" video.*

The American airplanes, in collaboration with their agent of the Jews and the Crusaders, Musharraf, launched an airstrike on Damadola near Peshawar around the Eid al-Adha holiday, during which 18 Muslims -- men, women and children -- died in their fight against Islam, which they call terrorism. Their claim was to target this poor man and four of my brothers. The whole world discovered the lies as the Americans fight Islam and the Muslims. Before I discuss this incident, I have some messages to send out.

My first message is to the butcher of Washington, Bush: You are not just defeated and lying about it, but you are, with God's help, a loser. You are bad luck to your people. You brought them disasters and catastrophes, and you will bring them even more disasters.

Bush, you failed crusader, know that we are the nation of monotheism, which believes that no one is greater than God. He sent us a prophet and a book that was never edited like the other books before it. A unique book that defies anyone to come up with anything like it.

I will meet my death when God wishes. But if my time hasn't come, you and all the Earth's forces can't change it, not even by a second.

Bush, do you know where I am? I am among the Muslim masses enjoying their care with God's blessings and sharing with them their holy war against you until we defeat you, God willing.

My second message is to the American people who are drowning in illusions. I tell you that Bush and his gangs are shedding your blood and wasting your money in frustrated adventures. The lion of Islam, Sheikh Osama bin Laden, offered you a decent exit from your dilemma, but your leaders, who are keen to accumulate wealth, insist on throwing you in battles and killing your souls in Iraq and Afghanistan and, God willing, on your own land.

Your leaders responded that they do not negotiate with terrorists and that they are winning in their war on terrorism. I tell them, O' liars and greedy war merchants, who is pulling out of Iraq and Afghanistan, you or us? Whose soldiers are committing suicide out of desperation, you or us?

To the American mother I say, if the defense ministry called you to tell you your son is coming back home in a coffin, remember Bush.

To the British wife I say, if you got a call telling you your husband is coming back home with his body paralyzed, amputated or charred, remember Blair."

## Dr. Ayman al Zawahiri
### March 4, 2006

I will start first by giving my condolences to the victims of the Egyptian Ferry, Al Salaam 98. And I ask God to give forgiveness to those killed, cure the injured and give them patience in their misery.

This major catastrophe shows the corruption in our countries that live under the shadow of treacherous regimes that were imposed on us by America to spread vice and filth in our countries, America that makes fighting Islam, torturing our people, despising our lives and sacred beliefs its law and way of life.

That clearly shows that as long as these governments stay in power, lives will be wasted, rights will be limited and corruption will be spread everywhere. The only solution and response should be Jihad because it is the only way to overthrow these kinds of governments in order to establish an Islamic rule that will respect the rights and honors of its citizens, fight corruption and spread justice and equality.

Secondly, I want to talk to you about the crusaders new hatred against Islam by the crusaders coalition led by America against Islam. One of its examples was the continuous wave of insults against the character of the blessed prophet may peace be upon him. They insulted the prophet may peace be upon him and they meant to continue this campaign of insults refusing to apologize. They did it on purpose and they continue to do it without apologizing, even though no one dares to harm Jews or to challenge Jewish claims about the Nazi Holocaust nor even to insult homosexuals or they would be criticized and legally prosecuted

The insults against Prophet Muhammad are not the result of freedom of opinion but because what is sacred has changed in this defeated culture. The Prophet Muhammad, prayers be upon him, and even Jesus Christ, peace be upon him, are not sacred any more, while Semites and the Nazi Holocaust and homosexuality have become sacred

In France, a law was issued to prosecute anyone who doubts that the Nazi Holocaust against the Jews didn't happen while they forbid muslims to wear the veils in their public schools. In France, a Muslim father cannot prevent his daughter from having sex because she is protected by the law, but this same law punishes her if she covers her hair.

And in England, they punish those who encourage Terrorism, yet, no one dare to punish those who are insulting our prophet. These insults against the prophet are a series of well planned insults by the crusaders against our Islam & Muslims. Did we forget Salman Rushdie and his ill criticism of the Prophet and the mothers of the believers? Did we forget how he is well received and honored everywhere he goes?

They even received him and welcomed him in the White House? Did we forget France's ban against the veil in the name of moderation? Did we forget the continuous desecrations by the Americans against our holy Quran? Did we forget how America pressured the Egyptian government to hand over the Muslim convert Waffa Constantine and her sisters back to her Coptic parents so she can suffer in their torturing dungeons, in the Coptic convents that are well protected by the Americans and the crusaders

And here is an Italian minister coming to Parliament wearing a t-shirt with the senseless cartoons that offend our prophet.

And here are the pictures of Abu Ghraib coming out again to show the American lies and criminal acts, that they claim that these are sprawling acts committed by a small number of soldiers, In war, they allow themselves to do everything they want. They invade our land, rob our wealth and then they insult us, insult our religion, our faith and our prophet then they come back to give us lectures about freedom, equality and human rights.

But we cannot fight these insults by demonstrations and burning embassies alone then going back and living our daily lives as we used to before. This will not be worthy enough for the great value of the Prophet peace be upon him. (Reading Quran)

But in order to face these insults, we need to rise as a one nation, to fight the crusaders campaign against Islam in everything that we have. But we have to ask ourselves, are we ready to sacrifice ourselves and everything that we own for the glory of God or do we only care about this materialistic life instead of caring about our own faith.

If we are ready to sacrifice ourselves and all what we have in the name of God, we have to be serious on getting ready to defend and fight against this crusader campaign that is targeting our religion and sacred beliefs, our lands and wealth, we need to carry on the fight on four related fronts:

The first front is to inflict losses on the western crusader , especially to its economic infrastructure with strikes that would make it bleed for years. The strikes on New York, Washington, Madrid and London are the best

examples for that. In this front, we have to deprive the western crusader from stealing the Muslims' oil which is being drained as the biggest robbery in history. And we have to boycott countries where satirical cartoons of the prophet Mohammad had been published including Denmark, Norway, France and Germany. And against all countries that participated in this war against Islam and Muslims.

In the second front, we have to get crusaders out of the lands of Islam especially from Iraq, Afghanistan and Palestine. The occupying forces must pay a heavy price for their invasion and they should get out of there as losers from our lands and after their economy totally collapse so we can establish in our lands the Islamic caliphate in god's willing. Every Muslim country everywhere around the world needs to contribute its resources for jihad wherever Jihad is needed against the crusaders and the Jews. Muslims need to rush for Jihad and contribute everything they have of weapons, finances, efforts, men and expertise. No one can imagine that Muslims should direct their funding, expertise and efforts anywhere else before we reach our goals in these fields first.

Our Mujahedeen in Iraq, Palestine and Afghanistan are our first defense line fighting for Islam and all Muslims. If this defense line is crushed, God forbids, the crusaders will be able to take over all our wealths.

The third front is working at changing the corrupt regimes [in our countries], which have sold their honor to the Crusading West and befriended Israel. Scholars and the influential should gather and consult with each other to take on the responsibility of changing these corrupt regimes. There is no hope in those governments as long as they insist on their position.

The fourth front is popularizing the Dawah [inviting non-Muslim to accept the truth of Islam] work. Every person who does that, along with every writer and scholar in the Muslim land should take part in enlightening Muslims about the dangers that face them, guide it to truth about Islam and taking up its Sharia, and warning them from every other agenda that rejects Sharia – even if it was made to look Islamic. They also should encourage Muslims to support the mujahedeen financially and psychologically. They should be good examples in their sacrifices of delivering the truth so that other Muslims can respond positively to those sacrifices.

Prophet Muhammed, peace be upon him, was asked 'What is the best Jihad [struggle]?'

He said, 'Saying what is truth and justice before a corrupt and unjust ruler.'

They should spread the religion in way that the Prophet described in the degrading realities that we are living until the Dawah [invitation to accept the truth of Islam] becomes a strong current that wipes out corruption among Muslims.

It is in these ways that we can effectively and realistically confront this Spiteful Crusade.

Perhaps these recent successive events have clarified to Muslims what kind of freedom the West wants for them. It is freedom of attacking Islam and Muslims. If these Crusaders take over our lands, as they plan to do so, they would have desecrated all that is sacred. Nothing will prevent these plans from coming true except the martyrdom and sacrifices of the mujahedeen. That's in Palestine, Iraq, Afghanistan and Chechnya. Without these majahedeen, we would have been in even worse situation.

O' Muslims, the West's principles and morals are hypocritical, believing that what is lawful for it is unlawful for anyone else. They think it is fine to bomb us and kill our women and children, but off limits for us to respond. They also think is fine to destroy and storm mosques in Afghanistan and Iraq, but it is not okay for us to know what is going on in torture places in so called Monasteries... Bush said in his last speech that the future of the United States depends on its fight against injustice and terrorism. But the U.S. did not and does not realize its real interests here. The U.S. is spreading injustice at the hands of its friends like Sharon, Musharraf, Mubarak, Abdullah ibn Hussein, and Zain el-abdeen bin Ali.

Bush is not spreading human rights either. Instead, he is spreading secret prisons everywhere, practicing mean torture in Baghram, Abu Ghraib and Guantanamo. He sends Muslims to be tortured in prisons belonging to his friends. Bush lied in his State of the Union speech when he said that the great Egyptian people have voiced their [true] opinions in the last presidential elections. The whole world knows how the Egyptian presidential elections were conducted – through forgery and criminal ways.

Bush, who claims to be a defender of democracy, has threatened Hamas in the same speech with stopping aide in case it does not recognize Israel, give up its struggle and abide by the agreements signed between Israel and the Palestinian Authority. AN in this context, it is important to warn my brothers in Palestine from a few things so they would understand the dimensions of the American conspiracy against them.

The first thing is that reaching power should not be used to submit to those conditions. Reaching power should be used to apply God's law in the land. So if we give up Sharia, how can God's law be applied! Applying God's law is one of the fundamentals of believing in One God [the main and first principal in Islam]. Taking up other laws, is not a part of our religion. It is another religion, and another sharia. [Quranic verse]

The second matter is that we must understand the realities and dimensions of the conflict. The reality of the conflict is that the Israeli occupation of Palestine is in the forefront of the Crusaders' mission against Islam and Muslims. The dimensions of the conflict include the confrontations between the world-wide Muslim community on one side and the Christian West on the other side. So Palestine is the worry for all Muslims. It is impossible to do jihad [struggle] there with a narrow and secular nationalistic way of thinking, which pushes aside Sharia and respects the seculars' influence in Palestine. On the other hand, every Muslim in Palestine is a part of the world-wide Muslim community and is responsible for supporting all of this community's issues.

The seculars in the PA have sold Palestine. Recognizing and legitimizing [their powers] is against the way of Islam. In the eyes of Islam, they are criminals. Palestine does not belong to them, nor is it a property that they can simply abandon. Sharing one legislative council and regarding their position of selling Palestine, which is against Islam, as a legitimate stand while accepting that the final judge between us and them is the number of votes is a clear opposition of Quranic teachings.

If we accept their authority and their system, then we've accepted their signed agreements. This also means if those criminals win majority in any future elections, then we will have to accept their position of selling out Palestine. It is not the right of any Palestinian or non-Palestinian to give up a grain of Palestinian soil.

It is a Muslim land that the disbelievers have occupied. And it is mandatory on every Muslim to attempt to return it to Muslim sphere.

It is very dangerous to accept to join these secular councils on the basis of a secular constitution, and on the basis of the Madrid, Oslo Roadmap agreements other agreements professing surrender. They are all against Sharia.

There are major references and principles for every nation. For example, the Jews do not

319

accept anyone who carries their passports to believe in the destruction of Israel and the U.S. Many other countries force their naturalized citizens to swear to respect their constitution and laws. Muslims have Islam as their reference. Its basis is believing in One God and submission to Him and His right to rule.

The third matter is that if we give the rule of Sharia in hopes of getting back a piece of Palestine, the Crusading West will not be satisfied. And it will continue to launch its war against us. It will not let us rule unless we accept what it is forcing us to do: recognition and surrender to Israel. So why sell our faith for the sake of materialistic rewards. We know very well that Palestine will not be liberated through elections but through struggle and Jihad for the sake of God.

The fourth matter: There have been a few official statements that accept and respect the agreements signed between the PA and Israel. This means that those who released those statements accept the Madrid, Oslo and Roadmap agreements along with others that admit surrender. This is a dangerous deal which should be dropped immediately.

One may wonder, for what gains has the Sharia given up? And for what gains has the surrendering agreements been accepted? Is it for 80 seats in Gaza?

My Muslim brothers in Palestine, Iraq and everywhere:

We must be cautious of the American game called the "Political process." This game is based on 4 deceiving things:

The first one is giving up Sharia as a rule of law.

The second is accepting the current situation and agreeing to surrender, which the enemy has forced it with those conspirators who sell out our honor.

The third is Disarming and leaving jihad behind.

The fourth is keeping the enemy on top while retaining its traditional and non-traditional armament. Its bases are our lands, the occupiers continue to bomb us transgress against us.

The Crusading-Zionist enemy entices some of us to be in power and lures them to accept some free-movement at the expense of agreeing to some of the conditions of the game. Then it pressures them to accept the test of the conditions. Therefore, we must confront the enemy's plot with a plan based on a creed of jihad, while holding on to the Sharia law and rejecting the agreements of surrender. We must continue the jihad and hitting its armament and its economic system.

Perhaps one may ask, what is the harm in achieving political gains, even if it's done in stages or little-by-little? The answer is that there is a heavy price to be paid for such moves. Is it for 80 seats in Gaza that our creed is lost and agreements of surrender are accepted?

Another person may wonder, what is the alternative?

The answer is that the alternative is the way of Prophets, Messengers, Dawah and struggle. We need to do Dawah [invitation to accept the truth of Islam] and jihad until the land is liberated and an Islamic state is established, God Willing.

O' my Muslim community everywhere, God (all Praise due to Him) did not order us to simply use any means to liberate the land, lift injustices, and protect all that is sacred. He specifically order us to do this through jihad [continued struggle] until the word of God is the highest and all faith is to Allah.

So if the faith is all to Allah and the word of God is highest, then earth is liberated, injustices are lifted, and all that is sacred is protected. But if we sacrifice our Sharia rule, and legitimized those who sell their nations and sign agreements of surrender, in hopes for liberating earth, alleviating injustice or protecting, then we will lose our faith and our lives. In the meantime, earth will still be occupied, injustices present and sacredness violated.

I conclude with a prayer of thanks to God, Lord of all worlds.

### To the People of Pakistan
### Dr. Ayman al- Zawahiri
### April 2006

In the name of Allah, and all praise is due to Allah, and may peace and prayers be upon the Messenger of Allah, and upon his family, companions, and allies.

Muslim brothers everywhere: peace be upon you and the mercy of Allah and His blessings.

The first thing that I want to talk to you about is the third anniversary of the American invasion of Iraq. We praise Allah that three years after the Crusader invasion of Iraq, America, Britain and their allies have achieved nothing but losses, disasters and misfortunes. They have become embroiled in Iraq in an unenviable way, despite Bush and Blair's continuous lying. And these losses and misfortunes only happened with the sacrifices of the Mujahideen and their enthusiasm for death in Allah's path. The group Qaida al-Jihad in the Land of the Two Rivers alone has carried out 800 martyrdom operations in 3 years, besides the sacrifices of the other Mujahideen, and this is what has broken the back of America in Iraq.

The sacrifices of the heroic Mujahideen have also exposed the total inconsistency of Western doctrine, and perhaps this moral and material defeat of the Western Crusade will motivate the West to review its ideological system in its entirety, if it desires the facts or hopes for salvation.

And just as the heroic Mujahideen's sacrifices have defeated the Crusader alliance morally and materially, they have also exposed the faction of traitors falsely associated with the Muslims, these traitors who made pacts with the Crusaders before, during and after the invasion, and prevented the Jihad against the occupation, and helped to establish it in Iraq, and promised it that they will be loyal guards of its interests after it leaves; they are traitors, even if they dress like the Muslims or have the same names; they are traitors, even if their beards are long and turbans great; they are traitors, even if they claim noble descent or a connection with the unseen or any other kind of charlatanism and superstition; they are traitors, and Allah, and His Messenger, and his righteous Companions, and pure People of his House, and the Islamic Ummah are innocent of them one and all. How can they claim affiliation to Islam when the Lord of Glory has given a verdict about them in His Book, saying,

By Laura Mansfield

"O ye who believe! Take not the Jews and the Christians for your friends and protectors: they are but friends and protectors to each other. And he amongst you that turns to them (for friendship) is of them. Verily, Allah guideth not a people unjust." Al-Maidah 5:51

Those who are in Iraq, and those affiliated to the clan of Hashim in Jordan, and their peers on the Arabian Peninsula, those who permit the recognition of Israel and making peace with it, and those like them in Egypt, who help France against the veiled Muslim women and receive the Israeli ambassador in noble al-Azhar and hand over Wafa Qistintin for torture in the dungeons of the monasteries: all of them are traitors, and the Muslim Ummah must confront them, lest they stab it from behind while it is exposing its chest to the rockets and bullets of the enemies.

As for the second thing I wish to talk to you about, it is the dark fate towards which the traitor Musharraf is pushing Pakistan. Without a doubt, Pakistan is one of the most important of the countries targeted by this new colonialist Crusade which seeks to weaken Pakistan and fragment it into entities under the control of India, which is allied with the Americans and Jews.

And here I wish to clarify an extremely important point, which is that the anti-Islamic

American/Crusader/Zionist plan has no place for the presence of Pakistan as a strong, powerful, able state in South Asia, because this plan doesn't forgive Pakistan for separating from India in the name of Islam, and doesn't forgive it for including the largest Islamic schools with wide influence among the Muslims of South and Central Asia, and doesn't forgive it for the flourishing of the popular Jihadi movements in it against the Indians in Kashmir and first the Russians and then the Americans in Afghanistan, and doesn't forgive it the favorable response of its people, scholars, students, Mujahideen and tribes to the Islamic Emirate in Afghanistan - since its founding and to this very day - and to its Amir the lion of Islam Mullah Muhammad Omar, may Allah protect him, and doesn't forgive it its overwhelming public sympathy for the call of Shaykh Usama bin Ladin for Jihad to expel the Americans and Jews from the holy places of the Muslims and their homes.

In this context, India appears to be the best candidate to implement the Zionist/Crusader plan to humiliate Pakistan and weaken it and tear it apart.

And Bush's recent visit to Pakistan at the beginning of March was one of the biggest pieces of evidence of that, as he gave a strong push to India's nuclear program while handing out orders and instructions in Pakistan. And I will review with you in brief just a few of the many woes and misfortunes which Musharraf and his supporters have brought upon Pakistan.

The first of these woes is Musharraf's combating of Islam in Pakistan. With an order from the Crusaders, he provided all the backing needed to expel the Islamic Emirate from Kabul. And he has made war on the Islamic schools, and is seeking to review the Hudood Act, in addition to inventing - with Crusader guidance - a new Qadiani creed which invites the people to an Islam without Jihad and without enjoining of good and prohibition of evil and without observation of the rules of the Shari'ah, which he calls "Enlightened Moderation."

The second of these woes is Musharraf's threat to Pakistani national security. Musharraf was the primary backer of the ouster of the Islamic Emirate from Kabul, and was the primary reason for the establishment of a government in Kabul allied to America and India and hostile to Pakistan. And as a result of Musharraf's betrayal, Indian intelligence has crept close to the Pakistan-Afghan border and opened its consulates in the cities adjacent to Pakistan. And the Pakistani Army, with the exit of the Taliban government from Kabul, became a double loser: first, the Pakistani Army lost the strategic depth which Afghanistan, with its highlands and mountains, can offer it in any Pakistani-Indian confrontation. And second, the Pakistani Army's back became exposed to a regime hostile to it and allied with its enemies. And if you add to this India's success in exploiting air bases in Tajikistan and its seeking military cooperation with the Central Asian states, you will realize the extent of the predicament which the Pakistani Army has gotten itself into.

And Musharraf is the one who placed the Pakistani nuclear program under American - and hence Jewish and Indian - supervision. Musharraf exploited America's accusation of Abdul Qadeer Khan to impose its surveillance upon the Pakistani nuclear program.

And then is it credible that Abdul Qadeer Khan was outside the surveillance of Pakistani military intelligence? Thus, the first ones who should be brought to trial in the case of Abdul Qadeer Khan are the leaders of the Pakistani Army and intelligence. But Abdul Qadeer Khan was used as a scapegoat to please America.

And Musharraf is the one who is fanning the flames of civil war in Pakistan on behalf of

America, in Waziristan and Baluchistan, in a bloody conflict whose losses have no end, and which will only rebound on Pakistan with the worst of damages.

The worst thing any army in the world could wish for is that it be assigned to defend the borders of its country at a time when it is embroiled in an internal civil war. Pakistani memory has yet to forget the catastrophe caused by the civil war in East Pakistan. And what Musharraf has done in Bajaur, Waziristan and Baluchistan, he will repeat in Karachi, Lahore and Peshawar, and indeed, any place the Americans request him to strike.

And Musharraf is the one who is seeking to change the combat doctrine of the Pakistani Army by repeating that the real danger to Pakistan is from within and not foreign: i.e., he is inciting the Pakistani Army to fight its people and brothers and turn a blind eye to the Indian threat. And if the combat doctrine of any army becomes corrupted, and its fighting turns into fighting for the sake of salary and position alone, then this army will run away from the battlefield whenever fighting breaks out.

And how is it possible for the Pakistani officer or soldier to be persuaded that he is defending Islam when he is the one who enabled the Americans to kill tens of thousands of Muslims in Afghanistan, and enabled them to oust the Islamic Emirate from Kabul? And how is it possible for the Pakistani officer or soldier to be persuaded that he is defending the sanctity of Pakistanis when his commanders order him to kill women and children in his own country? And how is it possible for the Pakistani officer or soldier to be persuaded that he is defending the honor and dignity of Pakistan when he sees his leaders order him to carry out a new slaughter every time they are visited by a high-ranking American official?

The third of these woes is Musharraf's squandering of the issue of Kashmir and his painstaking effort to dispose of it at any cost. Musharraf is the one who strangled the Jihadi resistance against India, which led it to increase its savagery and draw up the borders.

And Musharraf is the one who made and continues to make one concession after another in the Kashmir issue, even as India hasn't budged one step from its stance. And Musharraf is the one who seeks to deceive the Muslim Ummah in Pakistan by pretending to them that the problem with India will be resolved with confidence-building measures, in order to neutralize the effort to liberate Kashmir, which is the real problem between Pakistan and India.

And Musharraf is the one who wars against the Arab Mujahideen and their brothers from all corners of the Islamic world, who represent one of the most important weapons in the liberation of Kashmir, in the same way that they contributed before to the liberation of Afghanistan from the Russians.

And Musharraf is the one who brought American military and intelligence forces to Kashmir under the pretext of helping the victims of the earthquake. They came in under this cover and commenced to strengthen their defenses and fortifications in order to establish permanent Crusader bases on the Pakistani-Indian border.

The fourth of these woes is Musharraf's recognition of Israel, to psychologically prepare the Pakistanis to recognize a Hindu state in Kashmir.

The fifth of these woes is his affront to Pakistani dignity and sovereignty when he gave free reign to American intelligence and investigative agencies in Pakistan, and turned Pakistan's army and security services into hunting dogs at the service of the Crusaders.

The sixth of these woes is his corruption of political life in Pakistan. Through bribery and election fraud, Musharraf declared himself president and formed a party of bribe-takers and opportunists which he provided with a parliamentary majority, and distributed to them and the rest of his supporters the country's treasures, which he had seized, even though he is the same one who claimed at the beginning of his rule that he came to combat fiscal corruption in Pakistan.

And the West, which claims to defend democracy, was hostile to Musharraf at the outset of his rule, but later did a U-turn in admiration of him and his treachery, and indeed, today encourages him to stay in power at any means, after he demonstrated his aptitude for killing Muslims.

Musharraf's real problem is bribery. And Musharraf reckons that his success in procuring wealth will only be achieved by betraying Pakistan and appeasing America and throwing himself at its feet. But he forgets the other half of the reality, which is that America tosses its agents into the rubbish bin when there is no longer any need for them. And were he to look across his western borders, he would see the fate of the Shah bearing witness to that, when they ordered him to leave Iran, and then deprived him of asylum and indeed, even medical treatment, which he only found with his friend the bribe-taker Anwar Sadat.

And in keeping with Musharraf's worship of wealth and his mad dash for bribes, he tries to persuade the Pakistani people that they must take care of their interests without paying attention to any moral or religious considerations. This is the same logic of drug dealers, white slavery gangs, spies and traitors, and the outcome of this attitude is the loss of this world and the next. Allah the Exalted says, "Satan threatens you with poverty and bids you to immorality, while Allah promises you His forgiveness and bounties, and Allah cares for all and He knows all things."Al-Baqarah 2:268

I address the Pakistani people, to call on them to stand today in the ranks of Islam against the Zionist/Crusader assault on the Islamic Ummah and on Pakistan, and I call on them to strive in earnest to topple this bribe-taking, treacherous criminal, and to back their brothers the Mujahideen in Afghanistan with everything they've got until they defeat the plan of the Crusaders and Zionists allied with India.

I also call the Pakistani Army's attention to the dismal fate which awaits them in this life and the other, for the Pakistan Army has turned into forces aligned under Bush's cross in his Crusade against Islam and Muslims, just as it has become a tool in the destruction and tearing apart of Pakistan.

Let every soldier and officer in the Pakistani
Army know that Allah has threatened anyone
who allies himself with the infidels against the
Muslims with a painful punishment. Allah the
Exalted says, "To the hypocrites give the good
tidings that there is for them a grievous
chastisement; those who take for friends
unbelievers rather than believers: is it honor
they seek among them? Nay, all honor is with
Allah." Al-Nisa 4:138-139

And let every soldier and officer in the
Pakistani Army know that Musharraf is
throwing them into the burner of civil war in
exchange for the bribes which he took from the
Americans, and that he doesn't care if 10,000 or
20,000 Pakistani troops are killed, as long as his
pockets are full of bribes. And let them know
that Musharraf has made preparations to flee
abroad - where he has his secret accounts -
upon the victory of the popular revolution.

For this reason, I call upon every officer and
soldier in the Pakistani army to disobey the
orders of his commanders to kill Muslims in
Pakistan and Afghanistan, or otherwise he will
be confronted by the Mujahideen who repelled
the British and Russians before. The Truth -
Exalted is He - says, "Say to those who have
disbelieved, if they cease (from disbelief), their
past will be forgiven. But if they return

(thereto), then the examples of those (punished) before them have already preceded (as a warning). And fight them until there is no more fitnah (disbelief and polytheism) and the religion will all be for Allah alone (in the whole of the world) But if they cease (worshipping others besides Allah), then certainly, Allah is All-Seer of what they do. And if they turn away, then know that Allah is your Maula (Patron, Lord, Protector and Supporter) - (what) an excellent Maula, and (what) an Excellent Helper."Al-Anfal 8:38-39

And our final prayer is that all praise is due to Allah, Lord of the Worlds, and may Allah send prayers and peace upon our master Muhammad and his family and companions.

## Supporting the Palestinians
## Dr. Ayman al-Zawahiri
## June 2006

In the name of Allah, and all praise is due to Allah, and may peace and prayers be upon the Messenger of Allah and on his family, companions and allies.

Muslim brothers everywhere: peace be upon you and the mercy of Allah and His blessings.

I want to speak to you today about the Crusader/Zionist war against the Islamic world and its penetration into all aspects of our lives.

In Palestine, our Palestinian brothers are besieged to make them bow down and cause them to surrender completely to the will of the Crusader/Zionist powers of arrogance which seek to impose the Israeli presence in the land of Islam through armed force and the betrayals of the submissive rulers, from the ceasefire agreement of 1949 through the Oslo accord, the conference for the protection of Israel at Sharm el-Sheikh, and the Arab surrender initiative introduced by the custodian of the American doctrine of Tawheed [Abdullah ibn Abd al-Aziz].

And the Arab rulers – despite their extravagant spending on indecency, debauchery and security expenses for the subduing of the Ummah – didn't dare to meet the needs of the Palestinians for even one month, because orders were given by the Caesar of Washington to his regents to starve and blockade the Palestinians, and the Crusader West, Israel, and the Arab agents rushed to put them into effect.

And from the ironies in this regard is what was broadcast recently about Abdullah ibn Abd al-Aziz being the richest ruler in the world, as his declared assets amounts to 21 billion dollars: 21 billion dollars which he plundered and pillaged and took by oppressive force from the wealth of the Muslims, while the Muslims writhe with hunger. This is America's democracy and reform: does America dare to ask him, "From where did you get this?" Or is it the one who encourages, protects and supports him because the lion's share of this loot is poured into its banks?

Abdullah ibn Abd al-Aziz might argue that what was published was a lie. If so, then what is the truth? What is the size of your assets, and the assets of your sons, grandsons, relatives and brothers? Have you provided to the government a statement of financial liability in which you list your assets and holdings and how you procured them? And what are your allowances, and why do you take possession of them?

And are your assets subject to examination by an accountant or investigation by a court or monitoring by the people? And is there an independent body with immunity in charge of that? And is there an elected council which takes you to account for every riyal you earn or spend? Or is it that you have an army of scholars of beggary who make lawful for you the wealth, blood and sanctities of the Muslims because you are the Infallible Imam who plunders, oppresses, compromises, betrays, and rules, and whose order no one can refuse.

How, O Ummah, have you kept silent about this corruption in order for it to reach this degree of despotism? Were it not for our lust for life and hatred of death, this corrupt thief would not be ruling the Muslims in the state of doctrine and Tawheed. Isn't it our right to say to you, O Ummah, what Umar Abu Rishah said:

*Hold the complaints, for if it weren't for you*
*The slaves of the dirham would not here rule*

This is why I call on all Muslims everywhere to support their brothers the Palestinians, that support which must be directed first to the Mujahideen, then to the families of the martyrs and prisoners, and then, after the Mujahideen and families have been provided for, the remainder can be directed to the social and life-style aspects, in order for the Jihad to remain vital and effective.

And the backing of the Jihad in Palestine with one's self, wealth and opinion is compulsory on every single Muslim, because Palestine was an Islamic land which was occupied by the infidels, upon which its liberation and the restoration of Islamic rule to it became an individual obligation for every Muslim according to the consensus of the Ummah's scholars.

And such is the case with every land occupied by the unbelievers, and may Allah have mercy on the martyr of Islam – as we consider him – Shaykh Abdullah Azzam, who constantly repeated and affirmed that the Muslims are in sin from the fall of Spain until today, because they have not performed their personal duty of freeing the lands of Islam from the infidels.

As for our brothers in Palestine, I encourage them to hold to the creed of Tawheed and the rule of Shari'ah, and to refuse to recognize the secularist sellers of Palestine or recognize their presidency or authority, and to demonstrate a clear stance free of maneuvering and flattery by rejecting and refusing all accords of surrender and disowning them.

And I call on them to not lay down their weapons, because Palestine will never be liberated by begging help from the East and West nor by political gambits nor by recognizing the legitimacy of the sellers of Palestine and the sycophantic talk that avoids the facts, detours around the constants, and dissolves the stances of disassociation from the accords of surrender.

Instead, Palestine shall be liberated – with the permission of Allah – by the blood of the martyrs, suffering of the prisoners, and Jihad in the Path of Allah. And I also call on them to refuse any referendum on Palestine, because Palestine isn't for bargaining and bidding. Palestine was a land of Islam, and its liberation is the individual duty of every Muslim – all of Palestine, before and after 1967.

The cause of Palestine is one of the arenas of confrontation between the Muslim Ummah and the Crusader/Zionist assault, and isolating the Jihad in Palestine from the Muslim Ummah's Jihad against the Crusaders and their agents will only lead to loss of the religion and worldly life.

I am not asking those who isolate the Jihad in Palestine to perform Jihad in Chechnya – for example – but I request every Muslim in

Palestine to stand by the causes of his Ummah in Chechnya, Iraq, Afghanistan, the Philippines, and Guantanamo, even if it be with words or invitation or encouragement. Islam has never been nationalistic fighting in defense of political interests limited by national unity. Rather, Islam was and still is Jihad in the Path of Allah to protect and spread the creed of Tawheed. The Truth – Exalted is He – says, "And fight them until there is no more Fitnah [polytheism], and religion becomes Allah's in its entirety" 8:39 And the Truth – Exalted is He – says, "The believers, men and women, are protectors, one of another" 9:71 And the Truth – Exalted is He – says, "And if they seek your aid in religion, it is your duty to help them..." 8:72

As for Egypt, there the Crusader/Zionist assault backs the secular regime which attacks the impartiality of the judiciary and rigs the elections and imposes emergency laws.

And here I address the judges in Egypt, and I say to them: you shall not achieve your independence because America and Israel – simply and clearly put – don't want that. And what you seen today in terms of procedures against you is a part of the promised American reform project. And Jamal Mubarak was in Washington at the time of your protest to receive new backing from Bush for the policies of his father.

Judges: you shall not achieve independence in a subordinate, occupied homeland, and the regime shall not give you independence because he would by that be killing himself with his own hand.

But I must be frank with you and tell you that you are a part of the problem. You are pleased with the constitution and secular laws which were imposed on the Ummah by armed force and repression and torture and fraudulent elections.

And you are the ones who have helped to violate the rights of the nation; your hands write the rulings which devastate the Muslims, and with your hands, they are ruled by the emergency laws and laws of ruin and repression. And you know that the corruption of these laws is compounded by their being laws opposed to the Shari'ah as well as laws imposed by force and rigged elections, and yet you rule by them, and have not moved to object to them, although the judge Abd el-Ghaffar Muhammad admitted in the findings of his well-known decision that the constitution and laws clash with the Shari'ah which is absent from government in Egypt, and that the application of Shari'ah is the hope of every Muslim in Egypt.

And you know that the youth of Egypt and its free women and even its children are being severely punished next door to you, yet you haven't staged a sit-in nor taken to the streets. And you know that the prosecution colludes with the investigative services in the torture of Egyptians, yet you haven't staged a sit-in nor taken to the streets, nor demanded the disciplining of those who collude with the investigative services. And in the past, the accords of surrender were signed with Israel with fraud and deceit from a secular government which has usurped power, yet you didn't move, nor stage a sit-in, nor take to the streets.

And previously, Sulayman Khatir was killed in prison, yet you did not move, and the American forces moved out from Egypt to strike Iraq, yet you did not move. And the election took place with fraud and criminality, but you neither staged a sit-in nor took to the streets. And most of you agreed to participate in the drama of lies which you could have stopped. You took part in the elections, while you could have stopped this farce by refraining from continuing to participate in it, or by refusing to approve its results, or by issuing a report declaring its falseness and invalidity, even though the crimes and transgressions in it have affected you.

Is there any judge who dares to move to investigate the administrations of the state security services or police stations, which is within his authority legally? Is there any judge who dares to demand a sit-in to protest the absence of the Shari'ah from the government in Egypt, and to protest the presence of American bases in Egypt, and to protest the passing of warships through the Suez Canal to strike Iraq, and to protest the entrance of the Jews without visas to engage in corruption in the Sinai? Has any judge moved to stop the campaigns of mass torture in the Sinai?

Regrettably, you did not move when all these catastrophes occurred.

And you are regrettably a part of the secular regime which makes war on Islam and submits to America and Israel and rules its people through repression, theft, contrived constitutions, secular laws of ill repute, and rigged elections.

Judges: you shall only acquire independence in a free nation, and our homelands will only be liberated when the Shari'ah rules and the invaders are expelled and the tyrants are removed and the rights are returned to the Muslim Ummah. And without that, you are plowing in water and planting in the air.

If, however, you were to agree to sacrifice – in the path of Allah and in the path of truth and justice – your jobs and selves and wealth, then you would be victorious and your Ummah would be victorious with you, if only you acted on the Hadeeth of the Prophet, peace be upon him, "Truly, the best Jihad is a word of truth in front of an unjust ruler," and on the Hadeeth of the Prophet, peace be upon him, "The chief of the martyrs is Hamza ibn Abd al-Mutallib and a man who stood in front of an unjust leader and commanded him and forbade him then was killed by him." Then you would be victorious and your Ummah would be victorious with you. But without that, don't hope for independence or dignity or honor.

As for the extension of the emergency law in Egypt, I say to the Muslim Ummah: you shall continue to be suppressed and repressed so long as you don't liberate yourselves from the Crusade and its lackeys, no matter what this repression might be called: an emergency law or a terrorism law or a slavery law – the words are self-evident. And as long as this regime and its like in Algeria, Tunisia, the Arabian Peninsula, and Pakistan are sitting on your chest, you have no hope of salvation from the oppression and torture.

The only solution is to confront the tyranny and enjoin good and forbid evil and perform Jihad in the Path of Allah. We shall only be able to live in honor if we learn how to die as martyrs.

As for Libya, there the Crusader/Jewish assault has provided a certificate of distinction in treason to Qaddafi from the Caesar of Washington for his devotion to helping the Crusade against the Jihad. This, O our Muslim Ummah, is the democratic reform plan which Crusader America wants to impose on us through its executioners Qaddafi, Mubarak, Al-Saud, Musharraf and Bouteflika.

As for the Sudan, there the Crusader Security Council has decided to send military experts to Darfur to pave the way for its occupation and separation, and the treacherous Sudanese government participates with America in the division of the Sudan in order to preserve its hold on government.

This is why I call on every Muslim and on everyone in the Sudan in whose heart is a speck of faith and on everyone jealous for his Islamic religion in Darfur to stand in the face of this Crusader/Zionist plot to occupy the lands of Islam. It is incumbent that the differences with the Khartoum government not be made a justification for enabling the Crusaders and Jews to take the lands of Islam and Darfur. It is not possible for the call for liberation from the Khartoum government to be a justification for the enslavement of the Muslims at the hands of the Crusaders and Jews.

So may Allah grant long life to the Mujahideen everywhere, those who have confronted the Zionist Crusade led by America and severely injured it. And may Allah grant long life to the lions of Islam in Iraq, and may Allah grant long life to the patient champion of Islam, the Mujahid Abu Musab al-Zarqawi, and may Allah grant long life to the Shura of the Mujahideen in Iraq, and may Allah grant long life to every Mujahid and Murabit in Iraq of the Caliphate, and may Allah grant long life to the resolute, heroic Iraqi people: its leaders, scholars, tribes, and men and women who are confronting the Crusaders and their apostate helpers and the traitorous dealers in religion.

And may Allah grant long life to the people of Jihad and Ribat in Afghanistan, and may Allah grant long life to the Commander of the Believers, Mulla Muhammad Umar, who didn't sell his religion for worldly gain or because of his reign, and gave the entire world a lesson in Tawheed [Islamic Monotheism] and reliance [on God] and conviction. And may Allah grant long life to all the Mujahid and Murabit lions of Islam in Afghanistan who are aiding the religion of the Prophet, peace be upon him, in the face of the alliance of Crusaders and apostates.

I ask Allah to reward them well for their wholehearted campaign this spring, and I also ask Him – the Exalted – to make this summer a burning fire for the Americans and their Crusader allies and apostate agents. And may Allah grant long life to the lions of Islam in the towering Atlas Mountains, our brothers in the Salafist Group for Preaching and Combat defending Islam in Algeria in the face of the alliance of Crusaders and apostate traitor sons of France.

And may Allah grant long life to the lions of Islam in the defiant mountains of Chechnya, who have rubbed Russia's pride in the dirt. And may Allah grant long life to the lions of Islam in Palestine, Kashmir, Indonesia, the Philippines, Egypt, the Levant, the Arabian Peninsula and everywhere else, both those whom I have mentioned and those I have not, and those whom I have known and those whom I have not, those in whom I hope is realized the statement of the Truth, Exalted is He, "Among the believers are men who have been true to their covenant with Allah; of them some have died and some [still] wait; but they have never changed in the least." 33:23

The sacrifices of the Mujahideen haven't just foiled the plots of America against the Muslims, they have also thwarted its crimes against humankind, which is why I call on all the weak and oppressed around the world to stand with us in confronting the Great Satan and in confronting this criminal Western civilization which has committed outrages never before committed in the history of mankind, and to take advantage of the Mujahideen's attacks on America to rain their blows upon America until the symbol of tyranny in human history falls.

And our final prayer is that all praise is due to Allah, Lord of the worlds, and may peace and prayers be upon our Master Muhammad and his family and companions.

355

# J

Printed in the United States
59188LVS00003B/34